European Perspectives in Clinical and Health Psychology

Edited by

Chris R. Brewin
Department of Psychology
Royal Holloway and Bedford New College
University of London

Andrew Steptoe
Department of Psychology
St George's Hospital Medical School
London

Jane Wardle
ICRF Health Behaviour Unit
Institute of Psychiatry
London

Published by BPS Books (The British Psychological Society)
St Andrews House, 48 Princess Road East, Leicester LE1 7DR

Distributed by Plymbridge Distributors Limited,
Estover, Plymouth PL6 7PZ

The text of this volume also appears in the 'British Journal of Clinical Psychology',
Volume 31, Part 4, 1992

A catalogue record of this book is available from the British Library.

ISBN 1 85433 095 0

Printed in Great Britain by Cambridge University Press.

CONTENTS

*Page numbers refer to numbering in square brackets at the head of every page.

British Journal of Clinical Psychology (1992), **31**, 385   *Printed in Great Britain*

Introduction to the special issue

The move towards a single European currency and a single market, and towards the development of common policies on a wide range of social issues, together with the steady expansion of the European Community to include more and more countries, have created in Europe an unprecedented climate of mutual interest and desire for greater cooperation. This special issue is designed to reflect some of the benefits and opportunities that are now arising for clinical and health psychologists, and to create greater awareness of the richness of European research on a variety of important topics.

Some of these benefits derive from the investigation of cultural variations in clinical problems or psychological processes. Frequency data from different countries can highlight the relative importance of different symptoms, behaviours or cognitions. Our understanding of a phenomenon can only be enhanced by the knowledge either that it can be replicated in other countries or cultures or that the effect is specific to particular communities.

It is also illuminating to consider how explanations of the same phenomena vary across countries, and how completely different issues may be selected as being worthy of clinical and research efforts. The study of differences in health policy and service provision can provide a wealth of ideas for solving our own particular problems, enabling us to draw on a much wider range of innovative practices. There is also much of value to be gained from broadening our knowledge of the varied training and professional organization of European clinical and health psychologists.

The papers in this issue have been chosen to illustrate some of the insights and advantages that can accrue from taking a more pan-European perspective. Similar points could be made about other cross-national comparisons, and in future the Journal will particularly welcome submissions that draw on data from two or more different countries to illuminate aspects of either research or practice.

CHRIS R. BREWIN
ANDREW STEPTOE
JANE WARDLE

British Journal of Clinical Psychology (1992), **31**, 387–403   *Printed in Great Britain*

Post-traumatic stress disorders and European war veterans

Roderick J. Ørner*

Department of Clinical Psychology, North Lincolnshire Health Authority, Baverstock House, County Hospital, Lincoln LN2 5QY, UK

After tracing the history of PTSD as a diagnosis and exemplifying its use among non-European war veteran groups, this review article documents the size and characteristics of European war veteran populations and the known psychological, social and medical sequelae of war experience since 1918. Models of psychopathology vary markedly over time and between countries. Treatment practices owe more to sociopolitical and military expediency than systematic assessment of European veterans' needs and treatment outcomes. PTSD has not yet attained the pivotal status it enjoys in studies of American war veterans. Reasons for this are offered along with a proposal that recent European studies rightly highlight a broad spectrum of post-war adjustment difficulties in which PTSD emerges as a process phenomenon with implications for prognosis and future care planning,

One of the legacies of the Vietnam War is that clinicians worldwide have a fuller and more refined appreciation of the short-, medium- and long-term consequences of physically surviving the extraordinary threats of war. As a result of investigations carried out by the American Psychiatric Association Task Force on Nomenclature Statistics and recommendations made by Shatan, Haley & Smith (1977), a diagnosis of post-traumatic stress disorder (PTSD) was first introduced in the 1980 edition of the *Diagnostic and Statistical Manual of Mental Disorders* of the American Psychiatric Association. Representing a major conceptual shift compared to previous notions of 'gross stress reactions' and 'transient situational disturbance' featured in DSM (1952) and DSM-II (1968), the 1980 manual specified 12 symptoms that comprise the syndrome, described its acute, chronic and delayed manifestations, and allowed the presence of pre-morbid and other current pathology (Brett, Spitzer & Williams, 1988). During the first half of the 1980s the psychological sequelae of traumatization in war were more fully appreciated as were the wider repercussions on many aspects of personal adjustment (Figley, 1986). Also the diagnosis became associated with forensic, social and welfare policy issues (Blank, 1985; Marciniak, 1986), paving the way for PTSD to be used successfully as a criminal defence.

As part of its policy to monitor diagnostic practices the American Psychiatric Association established a subcommittee on post-traumatic stress disorder which undertook to revise DSM-III. Reflecting the subcommittee's conclusion that DSM-III criteria were fundamentally sound, the revised version (DSM-III-R) published in 1988 includes a description of generic characteristics of traumatic stressors as well as

* Requests for reprints.

Table 1. Wars within greater Europe since 1918 (excluding Second World War)

Year	Country	Parties involved
1918–20	USSR	Civil war. US, UK, France, Japan intervene
1919–19	Hungary	Czechoslovakia and Romania vs. Hungary
1919–20	Poland	USSR vs. Poland. French intervention
1919–20	Turkey	France vs. Turkey
1919–20	Hungary	Anti-communists vs. government
1919–22	Turkey	Greece vs. Turkey
1920–20	Lithuania	Poland vs. Lithuania
1934–34	Austria	Socialists vs. Fascist government
1934–34	Germany	Socialists vs. Nazi government
1934–34	Spain	Astorian miners vs. government
1936–39	Spain	Civil war. Italy, USSR, Germany intervene
1939–40	Finland	USSR and Finland
1945–49	Greece	Civil war. UK intervention
1956–56	Hungary	USSR intervenes in popular uprising
1977–80	Turkey	Terrorism, military coup 1980
1988–	Azerbaijan	Civil war. Armenian and Azerbaijani forces in Nagorno-Karabakh
1991–	Yugoslavia	Civil war.

Table extracted from Sivard (1987) and adapted.

symptoms of traumatic stress organized around the three core elements of intrusive re-experiencing, avoidance and numbing, and physiological arousal (Brett *et al.* 1988). In line with American Psychiatric Association policy future amendments to diagnostic criteria should be anticipated in DSM-IV.

Sustained by the insights afforded by DSM-III and DSM-III-R criteria for post-traumatic stress disorder, clinicians and researchers in the United States have established a track record of using this diagnosis in investigations of war veterans who survived the European and Asian theatres of the Second World War (Davidson, Kudler, Saunders & Smith, 1990; Hamilton & Canteen, 1987; Miller, Martin & Spiro, 1989) the Korean War (Druley & Pashko, 1988) and the Vietnam War (Stretch, 1986; Yager, Laufer & Callops, 1984). The same diagnoses have been employed in Australia by researchers investigating the prevalence of PTSD among Australian veterans of the Vietnam War (Boman, 1985) and in Israel (Bleich, Garb & Kotler, 1986). This paper reviews European studies which are promoting improved understanding of the plight of our war veterans and assesses the impact which the DSM-III and DSM-III-R diagnosis of post-traumatic stress disorder has had to date.

Veterans from which wars?

The World Veterans Federation has no reliable figures for the size and demographic characteristics of the war veteran population of greater Europe. Definition of a war veteran is in itself problematic. It needs to be broadened to include resistance fighters who operated within occupied countries, civilian prisoners of war and personnel who

Table 2. Wars involving European countries outside Europe since 1918 (excluding Second World War)

Year	Country	Parties involved
1918–18	Tibet	China vs. Tibet. UK intervention
1918–19	India	Amritsar massacre by UK
1919–19	Afghanistan	UK vs. Afghanistan
1920–20	Syria	France vs. Syria
1920–21	Iraq	UK vs. Arabs
1920–32	Libya	Italian conquest of Libya
1921–22	India	UK intervention in civil war
1921–26	Morocco	Civil war. France and Spain intervene
1924–25	Afghanistan	Anti-reformists vs. government. UK intervention
1925–27	Syria	France vs. Druse
1926–28	China	Civil war. USSR intervenes
1929–29	China	USSR vs. China
1930–32	Libya	Civil war. Italy intervenes
1931–34	China	USSR intervention in Turkistan
1935–36	Ethiopia	Italy vs. Ethiopia
1936–38	India	UK intervenes in civil war
1938–38	Japan	USSR vs. Japan
1939–39	USSR	Japan vs. USSR
1939–40	Syria	Egypt vs. Turkey. UK, Germany, France, USSR intervene
1940–41	Thailand	France vs. Thailand
1945–45	Algeria	Civil war. France intervenes
1945–46	Indonesia	Independence war. Netherlands and UK involvement
1945–54	Vietnam	Independence war vs. France
1946–48	India	UK intervention in civil war
1947–48	Madagascar	Independence war vs. France
1950–53	Korea	Korean War. UK, French involvement
1950–60	Malaysia	Civil war. UK intervention
1952–54	Tunisia	Independence war vs. France
1952–63	Kenya	Independence war vs. UK
1954–62	Algeria	Independence war vs. France
1953–56	Morocco	Independence war vs. France and Spain
1955–60	Cameroon	Independence war vs. France. UK involvement
1956–56	Egypt (Suez)	France, UK attack Egypt
1960–65	Zaire	Independence war. Belgium, UK intervene
1961–75	Angola	Independence war vs. Portugal. USSR involvement
1962–74	Guinea-Bissau	Independence war vs. Portugal
1963–72	Sudan	Black vs. government. UK intervention
1964–65	Bhutan	UK vs. Bhutan
1965–66	Indonesia	Abortive coup. UK intervention
1965–74	Mozambique	Independence war vs. Portugal
1969–69	USSR	China attacks USSR border
1974–74	Cyprus	Turkey vs. National Guard
1978–87	Afghanistan	USSR intervenes in civil war
1980–87	Chad	Rebels vs. government. French intervention

Table 2 (*cont.*)

Year	Country	Parties involved
1982–82	Falkland Islands	Argentina vs. UK
1987–88	Lebanon	UK, French troops stationed in Lebanon during civil war
1991–91	Kuwait/Iraq	War to liberate Kuwait. Most NATO countries involved

Table extracted from Sivard (1987) and adapted.

served or who are serving with United Nations peacekeeping forces. Since the Second World War when technological advances have played an increasingly important tactical role in major confrontations worldwide (e.g. aerial bombardment and air superiority), both soldiers and civilians have exposure to frontline dangers. With entire countries being transformed into battlefields the distinctions between military veterans and civilians is no longer valid. This is substantiated by the rapid rate of increase in civilian war casualties as a proportion of all killed. During the first half of this century this was 50 per cent rising to 52 per cent in the sixties, 73 per cent in the seventies and 85 per cent in the 1980s (Sivard, 1987).

The observation that no major war other than the Second World War has directly involved countries in greater Europe since 1918 belies the fact that armed conflicts which include one or more European governments and cause deaths of one thousand or more people per year have remained an almost continuous feature of every decade of our recent history. This is so with regard to wars within our continent (see Table 1), as well as engagements with nations in other parts of the world where in recent times our involvement is tending to become indirect or covert (see Table 2). The total number of people killed worldwide in wars, massacres and revolutions between 1945 and 1988 is between 15 and 20 million (Brogan, 1989). A measure of the impact of modern warfare on its participants is provided by Bartemeyer, Kobie, Menninger, Romano & Whitehorn (1946) who on the basis of available figures calculated an average attrition rate of 'one case of combat exhaustion and one death per five injured'. The number of European war veterans and civilians who continue to suffer some form of psychological impairment either on its own or in association with sustained physical injuries must extend beyond 10 million. The recent war to liberate Kuwait has added further to the number of personnel with experience of military service in a war zone.

The status of European war veterans

Five years after the First World War the International Labour Organization estimated the number of 'invalid soldiers who were receiving state pensions at over ten million'. France and Germany accounted for about 1.5 million disabled soldiers: over 80 per cent belonging to the 24 to 45 age group. In 1938 the British Government was still paying out almost half a million disability pensions to men wholly or partly disabled as a result of war service. Of these 25 000 received pensions for 'the after effects of shell shock'. At the time 3 200 patients were confined to 48 mental hospitals established specifically to provide psychiatric care for servicemen. In early 1980 27 000 disabled British servicemen were still receiving pensions for their First World War injuries. These figures quoted by van den Dungen (1981) are considered underestimates of the true casualty rate for conditions developing as a result of war operations between 1914 and 1918.

Compared to the 1914–1918 War relatively fewer physically disabled survivors resulted from the Second World War. All the same, in March 1948 413 000 Second World War veterans were receiving pensions or other financial assistance from the British Government. During that same year an accumulated total of 1.113 million war veterans and relatives in the United Kingdom were in receipt of some form of state assistance. In this war the countries of central and eastern Europe incurred the highest rates of military and civilian casualties. For instance the Federal Republic of West Germany paid financial benefits to over four million direct or indirect war casualties in 1956. This figure had reduced to 2.8 million by 1965 when 625 000 war veterans were assessed to have disabilities of 50 to 100 per cent.

As late as 1973 about 10 per cent of the population of West Germany had been exposed to extreme living conditions for several war years as POWs, civilian internees or concentration camp prisoners.

Conceptualizations of war-related traumatic stress in Europe (1914–1945)

For the greater part of this century mental problems of war veterans were perceived to result from the physical hardships endured such as disease, exhaustion and malnutrition. Although anxiety symptoms, depression and apathy were frequently reported, there was no generally accepted category of responses to war stress until the APA introduced PTSD in its 1980 diagnostic manual. The prevailing view during the late 1940s and early 1950s was that war veterans who resumed civilian status or were not hospitalized would either adjust without difficulty or recover physically and mentally during the immediate post-war years (Op den Velde, 1988). The early failure to reach nosological consensus about psychological reactions to war reflects the divergent views that prevailed not only about the aetiology and the nature of observed reactions to war experiences but also how treatment should be provided.

At the start of the First World War French psychiatrists assumed that reactions encountered in battlefield conditions would be consistent with those of patients seen during peacetime. Hysteria was therefore a common formulation in the initial stage but as the war progressed a number of new syndromes were described (hypnose des batailles, ruptus emotifs, ictus emotifs, puérilisme mentale). Eventually consensus emerged among French clinicians who described a syndrome of reactions called 'la confusion mentale de guerre'. Emotional shock assumed aetiological significance inasmuch as it was hypothesized to cause a release of toxic substances which accounted for mental confusion syndromes (Sutter, 1986).

The Anglo-Saxon perspective gave no centrality to mental confusion which was relegated to a minor element of 'shell shock'. This syndrome comprised a diversity of reactions including exhaustion, anxiety and conversion states. That these reactions should occur at all was typically explained in terms of 'faulty personality disposition' which pre-empted an efficient resolution of intra-psychic fight or flight conflicts.

Treatments were formulated with the implicit aim of resolving this conflict through abreaction and hypnotherapy as well as a variety of brutal methods as listed by Showalter (1987). She argues that the reason why a diagnosis of hysteria was hardly ever used in British or American military settings was that this particular condition had almost exclusively been attributed to women and explained in terms of alleged peculiarities of the female psyche. Ahrenfeldt (1958) has written a rich sourcebook reviewing the British armed forces' responses and reactions to traumatized personnel during two world wars, as perceived from within the medical corps. Among notable claims are that as early as 1917 the term 'shell shock' was being abolished at least in relation to physical injury, that special treatment centres were being set up to offer 'mental treatment' (Myers, 1940), and that modern treatment principles such as the therapeutic community and group therapy were developed by psychoanalysts in the British Army (Main, 1989). As to the quality and outcome of these evolving services no systematic information is offered.

By contrast, an early debate between organicists and psychogenicists in Germany culminated in the latter perspective becoming official doctrine. Psychological problems presented by war veterans were classified as a variety of hysteria resulting from psychological conflicts precipitated by battlefield conditions. Paradoxically this psychogenic formulation provided a pretext for introducing a series of repressive measures which would purportedly impact on the balance of conflicting psychological processes which, it was hypothesized, precipitated hysterical conditions. Special diets, isolation in dark rooms, prolonged immersion in water and electric shock were administered to soldiers in the name of treatment. As reported by Fischer-Homberger (1975) 'weak will power' was being treated with 'causal will therapy'. In 1918 Stern reported that in a sample of 300 combat veterans less than 2 per cent regained combat readiness. Alarm at the methods employed prompted the establishment of an Austrian official inquiry in 1920 which addressed the use of electric shock as a treatment for battle-induced conditions. No prosecutions resulted (Ellenberger, 1974).

In the build-up to the Second World War Nazi propaganda sought to foster a patriotic public well motivated and prepared for armed service. The advent of war nevertheless produced psychological casualties, who by Stoering's decree (1942) were to be diagnosed as 'war hysteria'. Individuals so classified were viewed as malingerers for whom official orders prescribed severe personal repression intended to instil regret. A high risk of suicide was acknowledged to be a consequence of this regime but this was to be no deterrent (Sutter, 1986).

During the Second World War a number of articles on traumatized war veterans were published in the UK and military clinicians linked delayed combat reactions to the psychosomatic complaints so prevalent among their patients. For instance Torrie (1944) outlines 2500 psychosomatic casualties incurred in the Middle East during 1942, and offers a more detailed description of 1000 patients with diagnoses of anxiety neuroses and hysteria. 'Pre-war neurosis' was reported for one quarter of the latter group of casualties. Londoners buried under debris for more than one hour without sustaining physical injury were followed up by Fraser, Leslie & Phelps (1942/43): 65 per cent developed clear-cut neurotic symptoms. Loss of a near relative or close friend was associated with severe symptomatology. Among these civilians only those with 'vulnerable personalities' were found not to recover within weeks of being bombed. As a treatment for civilians and soldiers alike narcoanalysis found continued use so the overall impression is of only minor conceptual progress since the First World War. It should be noted that notions of battle exhaustion or combat fatigue as introduced by the allies did not reflect improvements in psychological understanding of war experiences. The terms imply that combat would produce soldiers who are tired or exhausted and for whom the prescribed intervention was rest, quickly provided near the front lines in order to ensure a rapid return to combat units. Lefebvre (1982) claims that a review of military records in France documents that 11 800 servicemen were reformed from their mental problems using these methods.

Conceptualization of war-related traumatic stress in Europe since 1945

European nations came to a realization of veterans' post Second World War adjustment difficulties by a variety of routes. Refugees and concentration camp survivors were first targeted for systematic study during the late 1940s and early 1950s (Eitinger, 1958, 1964; Eitinger & Strøm, 1973, 1981), soon to be followed by sailors who had served on convoy duties in Norway's exiled merchant marine. Askevold (1976) identified them as a high risk group and coined the term 'war sailors' syndrome'. It consisted of fatigue, lack of initiative, irritability, somatic pain, impotence, physiological reactivity, personal and social isolation, nightmares, restlessness and sleep disturbance. Impaired memory and concentration difficulties were reported in nearly 90 per cent of the 120 war sailors studied. Significantly the syndrome was recognized as being strikingly similar to 'the concentration camp syndrome' first described by Helweg-Larsen, Hoffmeyer, Kieler, Hess-Thaysen, Thygesen & Wulff (1952). Given their chronicity and poor prognosis investigators had to acknowledge the very severe post-war adjustment difficulties experienced by an overwhelming majority of sailors with records of convoy duty between 1939 and 1945. Bastiaans (1957) has reviewed some of the articles which had appeared by the end of the 1950s linking severe mental disorder in war veterans to wartime violence. Typically, syndromes included vague complaints such as fatigue, poor concentration, irritability and insomnia.

German investigations into the psychological and psychoanalytic sequelae of prolonged war trauma have been published since the mid-1970s. In the main these reports are based upon test protocols and there are few methodical clinical studies (Böger, Schenck, Thürauf, Valentin & Weltle, 1975; Höpker, 1982; Paul, 1986; Schenck, 1975, 1976, 1979; Schenck, Scheidt & Goetz, 1984; Thürauf, Schenck, Valentin & Weltle, 1975).

This relatively early recognition of psychosocial and medical problems arising from war experience alerted Scandinavians to undertake long-term follow-up studies of their personnel serving with United Nations peacekeeping forces in Gaza (1956–63), Congo (1960–61), and South Lebanon (1979...). Ketner (1972) undertook a series of follow-up studies of 1086 Swedish personnel involved in the Congo conflict and 1242 controls. For this population there is no reported difference in either 'total psychological morbidity' or 'clear-cut mental illness'. Combat veterans showed a greater tendency towards accident proneness but on other personal, social, economic, health and employment variables combat veterans were indistinguishable from peer control groups. This held true also for 40 men posted in Africa who had responded with 'combat induced states of mental incapacity with characteristics resembling combat exhaustion'. The only discernible trend in this sample was that they tended to be among the younger members of the UN Forces. Other variables had no consistent relationship to long-term outcome which was equally good for all groups. Similar findings are reported in a more recent follow-up study of two Swedish United Nations Peacekeeping battalions who served in Cyprus during the years 1984–85 (Lundin & Otto, in press).

The risks of psychological traumatization arising from United Nations peace-keeping operations under conditions of military hostility have been assessed in South Lebanon since 1979. Weisaeth & Sund (1982) followed up members of the first contingents of United Nations soldiers who served in Lebanon. A particular kind of stress syndrome was reported characterized by fears of overaggressive responses. It is postulated that this was a consequence of rules of engagement stipulating that retaliation should be avoided even when under attack. Lundin & Otto (1989) reviewed Swedish experiences during a two-year period from 1982 and Carlstrom, Lundin & Otto (1990) have recently reported a high proportion of 'stress symptoms' in their sample of servicemen belonging to a Swedish logistic battalion in this part of the Middle East. All the same, adjustment of respondents to UN Service is said to be good. Low short- and intermediate-term morbidity is reported in a recent review by Weisaeth (1990) who incorporates in his analysis data available from UN peacekeeping personnel from Norway, Holland, Ireland and France. A warning of possible longer-term sequelae has recently been given by Aarhaug (1991) who reports that 400 Norwegians with service records in Southern Lebanon have presented with sleep problems, nightmares and obsessive–compulsive disorders. These symptoms often co-exist with physical symptoms of muscle tension, digestive tract problems and poor general health. Although notable for methodological sophistication and comprehensiveness it is only very recently that Scandinavian surveys have started to make DSM criteria for post-traumatic stress disorder central to their research projects.

Retrospective analysis of records gathered on Finnish soldiers between 1941 and 1944 (Ponteva, 1977) found psychogenic reactions to correlate with numbers of casualties incurred. The estimated casualty rate for non-physical injuries peaked at the beginning of the war and during the Russian great summer offensive in 1944. A 1971 follow-up revealed higher mortality and morbidity rates among the war veterans compared to non-combat veteran controls hospitalized with pneumonia. This was particularly so for cardiovascular diseases and disorders of the musculoskeletal system. Many veterans reported retaining their ability for civilian work for many decades after the war, but compared to controls a marked decline in work ability had begun in the early 1970s for the veteran group.

Among French troops serving in Indo-China 'a proportion became alcoholics and others manifested psychopathic reactions' (Sutter, 1986). The same author also summarizes the clinical impressions of traumatization in Algerian War veterans as 'a worsening of pre-military service difficulties consistent with personal predis-positions'. Sigg (1989) gives graphic descriptions of individual anguish and social unease in both France and Algeria which followed from the colonial war that cost more than one million lives. French troops serving in Biafra in 1968–69 showed a propensity to 'acute nervous decompensation'. During the 1980s 'confusion mentale de guerre' continued to be a preferred diagnosis in France reflecting local clinical perspectives which continued to draw heavily on psychoanalytic theory and practice (Barrois, 1984; Crocq, Sailhan & Barrois, 1983; Juillet & Moutin, 1969; Kammerer, 1967). This is illustrated by Crocq & Crocq's (1987) attempt to review interaction effects between premorbid personality and traumatic war experiences drawing upon material from the Second World War and the Algerian War. The authors stress that the vulnerability caused by past personality 'is not an unescapable fate' and that every traumatic neurosis has a trauma as its origin.

PTSD studies on European war veterans

Whereas the precarious psychological and physical state of European war veterans has been increasingly recognized since the mid-1950s (Bastiaans, 1957), no diagnostic categories have so far been included in the International Classification of Disorders in which the extreme stresses of service in a war zone are singled out as a discriminating aetiological variable. By contrast DSM-III and DSM-III-R have offered clinical investigators such a system of classification, prompting a number of studies into the prevalence of PTSD among European war veteran groups, notably in Holland, the United Kingdom and France.

It has taken nearly 10 years for studies of PTSD among British Falklands War veterans to be published. O'Brien & Hughes (1991) compared selected war veterans from the two parachute brigades who fought on these islands with the brigade that remained in Europe. Of those who were still serving as paratroopers 22 per cent were rated as having the complete PTSD syndrome. Continuing traumatic stress reactions were associated with intensity of combat experience and retrospective report of emotional difficulties in the initial period on return from the war. Meeting DSM-III criteria for PTSD was also associated with 'caseness' as assessed by the 60-item version of the General Health Questionnaire (Goldberg, 1978).

Ørner (in press) undertook a pilot survey of British ex-servicemen who served in the South Atlantic during the Falklands War. Ministry of Defence resistance to this project placed severe constraints on access to the war veterans, but in a report based on postal questionnaire returns from 53 Falklands War veterans, 63 per cent met DSM-III criteria for PTSD; chronic subtype. Compared to those Falklands War veterans not meeting diagnostic criteria, the former group reported poor general health as measured by Goldberg's General Health Questionnaire (Goldberg, 1978a), and had more social and personal adjustment problems. Typically these problems increased steadily over time but at a fluctuating rate. These surveys are the first to produce data on the prevalence of post-traumatic stress reactions and attendant problems in a new European war veteran population. Indications are that if Falklands War veterans are not followed up we shall emerge with incomplete impressions of the personal and social costs of sending young men into battle and then neglecting their short-, intermediate- and long-term needs. The implications of such a failure in a society's duty to care are exactly those highlighted by Op den Welde (1988) for a different veterans' group.

As part of a larger study Op den Velde *et al.* (1990) reported on the prevalence of current PTSD in a sample of Dutch resistance veterans. Severe traumatization does not preclude apparent good or even excellent social and professional functioning for considerable periods of time through adult life. Resistance group veterans were found to retire earlier than peer group controls and a significantly larger proportion were eligible for disability pensions at the time of retirement. PTSD symptoms grew worse after retirement. The post-war adjustment histories of these resistance workers revealed more marital problems, more educational difficulties for their children and a higher divorce rate. Three distinct developmental courses for PTSD over the life-span were found. Acute PTSD would persist to become a chronic state; delayed onset following a symptom-free period lasting between five and 35 years; and a fluctuating course with symptoms manifest for five years after the war followed by symptom-free intervals of 15 to 30 years after which PTSD symptoms recurred. Those not meeting the criteria for a differential diagnosis did, however, report insomnia and intensification of distress after exposure to events that reminded them of or resembled their war experiences. The prevalence rate of PTSD did not differ significantly between those resistance veterans who endured uninterrupted emotional tension by remaining active until the ceasefire in 1945 and those who were arrested, interrogated and imprisoned in concentration camps. Both groups reported poorer physical health status than same-age controls from the general Dutch population.

More recent analysis of scores achieved on psychometric assessment for anxiety, depression and anger in resistance veterans and control groups (Hovens, Op den Velde, Falger, Schouten, De Groen & van Duijn, in press) confirm earlier findings of PTSD sufferers experiencing particularly pronounced functional impairments. The authors argue that high scores on anxiety, depression and anger are not unique to traumatized individuals. Other subjects with anxious and depressive symptomatology achieved a similar pattern of scores, but only the resistance veterans reported intrusive reminiscences of stressful events among their symptoms.

In 1988 a postal survey questionnaire was sent to about 2000 members of La Fédération des Anciens de Tambow et Internés eb Russie (Association of Survivors from Tambow and other Russian POW Camps). Replies received from 817 members were analysed and reported by Crocq, Hein, Duval & Macher (1991): 71 per cent experienced enough symptoms to meet DSM-III-R criteria for PTSD. Duration of imprisonment was strongly linked to a positive diagnosis as was the severity of experiences during captivity. These included malnutrition, being wounded, actual torture and being threatened with death. These stressors proved to be more powerful predictors of current PTSD than a simple measure of time spent in captivity.

Evolving alternatives to PTSD in Europe

Throughout Europe there is no broad recognition that war service is likely to have consequences for future personal, social and health adjustment of the individuals involved. Op den Velde (1988) argues that this is attributable to technological developments which have so fundamentally changed the manner in which modern wars are fought and the increasing involvement of civilian populations in the horror and extensive damage that results from military hostilities.

From observations of a large number of survivors Dutch investigators have adapted the concept of 'vital exhaustion' to their assessment of long-term traumatic stress reactions. This term was originally derived from psychosocial research with cardiac patients who in the months and weeks prior to a first coronary event reported having experienced a particular psychological and physical state characterized by feelings of arousal, tiredness and general malaise. Such a state occurs most commonly among those who are faced with life-crises or with a prolonged period of work overload. Although the state may be transient it placed individuals at high risk for disease onset. This is especially so if a patient already has a medical history suggesting somatic deterioration (Appels, Höppener & Mulder, 1987). Dutch investigators have demonstrated how chronic traumatic stress symptoms, as described in DSM-III and DSM-III-R, both maintain and mediate the pathogenic processes that culminate in vital exhaustion, reduced capacity for adjustment to the stress of everyday life, poor health and failure to regain good health. This is described in more detail in a study by Rosen & Fields (1988).

Falger, Op den Velde, Hovens & Schouten (in press) have reported a study which demonstrates the insights to be derived from the Dutch perspective on PTSD as mediating and maintaining chronic psychological, behavioural and somatic problems. They explored the relationship between PTSD, vital exhaustion and a number of clinical, behavioural and psychosocial risk indicators for coronary heart disease in a sample of 147 Dutch Second World War resistance veterans. These war survivors were compared with 65 male patients with first myocardial infarction and 92 male hospital controls who had participated in an epidemiological survey about life-span developments and first myocardial infarction (Falger, 1989). Fifty-six resistance veterans who were between 15 and 24 years old during the Second World War were suffering from current PTSD. Sleep disturbance and hyperarousal were the most frequently reported symptoms. These veterans were described as 'vitally exhausted to an unusual degree' as assessed by the Maastricht Questionnaire (Falger, 1989) when compared to recent myocardial infarction cases. The veteran group showed a higher occurrence of Type A behaviours. Hospital controls sampled from the epidemiological survey had significantly fewer symptoms of angina pectoris and hypertension than their peers in the resistance veteran group. Regression analysis revealed veterans suffering PTSD to differ from those who did not meet the diagnostic criteria on two main factors: 'current vital exhaustion' and a pre-war stressor described as 'prolonged financial problems in childhood and adolescence'. The study confirms strong links between traumatic war experiences, current PTSD, vital exhaustion and the presence of behavioural, psychosocial and clinical risk indicators for coronary heart disease.

It is now clear that traumatic nightmares and sleep disturbance are prevalent in groups of war veterans in the Netherlands. In a study of 30 current PTSD subjects night sleep was characterized by less total sleep time, diminished sleep efficiency, decreased REM latency, and a decrease in stage III/IV sleep. The data also suggest that nightmares could be triggered by sleep-apnoeic episodes (De Groen, Op den Velde, van Duijn, Falger, Hovens & Flos, 1990).

Based on clinical experience with at least 500 war survivors De Loos (1990a) categorized the long-term psychosomatic sequelae of chronic PTSD into five groups. A state of chronic arousal, sustained by fears arising from near-death experiences and classical conditioning to war-related stimuli, leads to disturbances at a psychosocial level. Its most frequent manifestations are phobias, anxieties, depression and exhaustion. A second category of sequelae consists of somatoform reactions like conversion states, hypochondriasis and psychogenic pain. Patients may be consciously unaware of the link with past traumatic experiences which find expression through troublesome bodily reactions. The longer-term consequences of a conditioning history where fight or flight responses have been evoked regularly during extended periods of wartime service, are seen in a range of neuropsychological (depersonalization, blurred vision), circulatory (angina, tachycardia), neuromuscular (tremor, tension headaches, muscle weakness), digestive (abdominal pain, acute diarrhoea), respiratory (breathlessness, hyperventilation) and other symptoms such as acute fever, perspiration, urges to urinate and skin exanthema. Central to all these presentations is a chronically established psychophysiological state of arousal expressed psychologically as anxiety. A fourth category of reactions are those frequently occurring somatic diseases found among Second World War survivors (cardiac, skin, pulmonary, gastrointestinal and 'various other' conditions) which, once manifest in the patient group, are associated with increased morbidity, in all main diagnostic categories and higher mortality in a distinct group of diseases (Eitinger & Strøm, 1981).

None of these categories is entirely distinct, so further complications arise through behavioural–somatic interactions. Heavy smoking or drinking is a case in point, as is the difficulty experienced by many traumatized individuals in following advice concerning diet, life-style and medication. De Loos (1990a) advocates great caution in the use of medications for these conditions. The dangers are that the prescription of medicines may reinforce somatization of emotional problems and make patients less amenable to other appropriate therapies, whether medical or psychological. Given the complexity of the clinical pictures presented by chronically traumatized war survivors it is not uncommon for the clinical situation itself to induce feelings of anxiety and helplessness. Flexibility and a readiness constantly to review patient care is a prerequisite to ensuring that comprehensive psychological and medical assessments are followed by multidisciplinary treatments. De Loos (1990a) advocates that staff providing care for war veterans require specific peer support networks to reduce risk of burnout and vicarious traumatization. Two case studies published by De Loos (1990b) illustrate some of the points made above.

Op den Velde (1988) elaborates these complex issues by questioning the impression that apparently successful post-war adaptation is achieved without severe mental complaints. He argues that, during this long latency period, a range of subtle and accumulating changes in mental functioning do in fact occur. Inability to experience emotions, feelings of alienation, isolation, profound distrust and excessive activity are most common. For instance, matrimonial problems reflecting a broader disturbance in relationships are encountered more often among war victims who may also harbour a menacing feeling of disappointment in post-war social developments.

Concluding observations

Europe enjoys a history of recognizing psychological sequelae of wartime experience that spans more than two millennia (Trimble, 1985). The clinical literature published to date is remarkable for the varied perspectives put forward to account for these reactions. Consequently, there has been an absence of agreement in diagnostic practice throughout the continent at any one time. Striking inconsistencies are also found within particular countries during different phases of their recent history. The overriding impression is of clinical practice being steered by socio-political and military expediency. In wartime the pervasive influence of violence permeated treatment perspectives which, with the benefit of hindsight, owed little to critical assessments of veterans' psychological needs. The present author has been unable to find a single controlled study of treatment outcomes carried out with European war veterans. In this light Op den Velde's (1988) reports of disillusionment, alienation and resentment among war veterans should be registered as serious complaints rooted in factual failure to meet the needs of people with records of war service. Europe's legacy appears to be one of not having conducted any comprehensive, methodologically sound investigations that adequately describe post-war functioning and adjustment among its older and more recent war veteran groups. The few reports published to date tend to focus on a limited number of functional impairments discovered in small veteran populations. This is in sharp contrast to the United States where a number of comprehensive projects have been completed which clarify the current psychological, social and medical status of its now numerous war veteran groups (Wilson, Harel & Kahana, 1988).

Any consideration of how Europe should proceed must start with an appreciation of contextual differences between the United States and Europe. In the 1960s and 1970s the former found itself with a larger number of new, young, active war veterans with service records from South East Asia. They forced a reluctant public into awareness of difficulties encountered after demobilization (Emerson, 1976). This raises important questions about the possible appropriateness and discriminative power of the PTSD diagnosis amongst those who are survivors of wars that ended much earlier this century. Dutch researchers draw attention to vital exhaustion (Falger *et al.*, 1990) and psychosomatic disorders (De Loos, 1990*a*, *b*) as pervasive aspects of the clinical picture presented by older veteran populations with PTSD. In DSM-III-R these impairments are referred to as 'co-morbidity'. European evidence, however, suggests that chronic psychological and physical impairments are mediated by a syndrome of reactions that conform more or less to the diagnostic entity of post-traumatic stress disorder (Hovens *et al.*, in press), and that current PTSD status emerges as a powerful psychological, medical and social prognosticator. This is especially so in the long term (Falger, 1989).

Implied in the above is the possibility that post-traumatic stress reactions may more usefully be considered to be phenomena associated with adjustment processes. Acute reactions to traumatic events are an integral part of the complex adjustment process which often culminates in a point of resolution where aspects of critical incidents are incorporated into existing schemata. Horowitz (1990) has described such a process model for bereavement, the key elements of which transfer to the psychological processing of war trauma. Chronic PTSD as reported by European war veterans can therefore be postulated to indicate a failure, or the impossibility of, processing past experiences. This will result in an almost permanent homeostatic disequilibrium as described by De Loos (1990*a*). Functional impairments, poor general health and vital exhaustion ensue. It is therefore possible that acute PTSD reactions provide clinicians with a model of how critical or traumatic events are processed psychologically towards a point of resolution. Chronic and delayed manifestations indicate a failure to process war experiences. This results in impaired functioning and predicts high rates of mobidity and mortality in years to come.

In Europe it is also necessary to address questions that may be asked about the discriminative value of a PTSD diagnosis on its own. Crocq *et al.* (1991) and Ørner (in press) report point prevalence rates in excess of 70 per cent and 60 per cent for French prisoners of war and demobilized Falklands War veterans respectively. This points to the limitations of the accepted dichotomous system of classification. Future research in Europe should therefore establish how PTSD diagnosis is associated with other measures of psychological, social and medical functioning. A further requirement is that studies must incorporate long-term monitoring of change with a keen eye on variables such as intensity of traumatization and the clinical or personal impact of the psychological reactions reported by the veterans. To date no tools have been published which validly and reliably assess such qualitative aspects of traumatic stress reactions. Once these become available light might be thrown on the processes which promote apparently successful post-war adjustment by some veterans whilst others remain permanently incapacitated.

As currently conceptualized in DSM-III-R differential response to traumatic war experiences is accounted for by intensity and duration of the stressor (Green, Grace, Lindy & Gleser, 1990). A recent study by Feinstein & Dolan (1991) points to a need to qualify this perspective. They found post-accident distress closely linked to difficulties of cognitive assimilation of the traumatic event. In turn this proved highly predictive of future psychiatric morbidity and chronic PTSD. If substantiated by other studies, results verify a need to review the DSM-III-R conceptualization of traumatic stress reaction as disorder. A synthesis incorporating the European trend to view PTSD as process and prognosticator will promote a more enlightened view of problems experienced by war veterans. It will also inform clinical professions in the continuing search for effective care and support programmes.

In conclusion, therefore, studies of European war veterans published to date reveal how little reliable and valid knowledge we have about this large population found in all parts of our continent. Those populations that have been sampled and studied are generally encumbered by higher morbidity and mortality than comparable non-veteran citizens. This scarcity of information remains a severely limiting factor for clinicians seeking guidance on how to plan and prioritize their therapeutic endeavours. However, as a consequence of having identified key elements in the syndrome of psychological and somatic reactions that follow in the wake of traumatic war experiences, we are, for the first time, on the threshold of moving from mere symptom description to a discovery of process variables which directly affect personal adjustment following exposure to the extreme violence of war.

References

Aarhaug, P. (1991). FN-soldater lider av senskader. *Aftenposten*, 2 June, p 4.

Ahrenfeldt, R. H. (1958). *Psychiatry in the British Army in the Second World War*. London: Routledge & Kegan Paul.

American Psychiatric Association (1952). *Diagnostic and Statistical Manual*, vol. I. Washington, DC: American Psychiatric Association.

American Psychiatric Association (1968). *Diagnostic and Statistical Manual*, vol. II. Washington, DC: American Psychiatric Association.

American Psychiatric Association (1980). *Diagnostic and Statistical Manual*, vol. III. Washington, DC: American Psychiatric Association.

American Psychiatric Association (1988). *Diagnostic and Statistical Manual*, vol. III, Revised Version. Washington, DC: American Psychiatric Association.

Appels, A., Höppener, P. & Mulder, P. (1987). A questionnaire to assess premonitory symptoms of myocardial infarction. *International Journal of Cardiology* **17**, 15–24.

Askevold, F. (1976). War sailor syndrome. *Psychotherapy and Psychosomatics*, **27**, 133–138.

Barrois, C. (1984). *Aspects de la Psychiatrie Militaire*. Paris: Val de Grace.

Bartemeyer, L. H., Kobie, L. S., Menninger, K. A., Romano, J. & Whitehorn, J. C. (1946). Combat exhaustion. *Journal of Nervous and Mental Diseases*, **104**, 359–389, 489–525.

Bastiaans, J. (1957). *Psychosomatische Gevolgen van Onderdrukking en Verzet*. Amsterdam: Noord-Hollandsche Vitgeversmaatschappÿ.

Blank, A. S. (1985). The Veterans Administration's Vietnam veterans outreach and counselling centres. In S. M. Sonnenberg, A. S. Blank & J. A. Talbott (Eds), *The Trauma of War: Stress and Recovery in Vietnam Veterans*. Washington, DC: American Psychiatric Press.

Bleich, A., Garb, R. & Kotler, M. (1986). Combat stress disorder and the military physician. An approach to a category of post-traumatic stress disorder. *Journal of Royal Army Medical Corps*, **132**, 54–57.

Böger, A., Schenck, E. G., Thürauf, J., Valentin, H. & Weltle, D. (1975). *Epidemiologische Studie über die Todesursachen ehemaliger Kriegsgefangener*. Nuremberg Studie. Stuttgart: Gentner.

Boman, B. (1985). Post-traumatic stress disorder (traumatic war neurosis) and concurrent psychiatric illness among Australian Vietnam veterans. A controlled study. *Journal of Royal Army Medical Corps*, **132**, 128–131.

Brett, E. A., Spitzer, R. L. & Williams, J. B. W. (1988). DSM-III-R criteria for posttraumatic stress disorder. *American Journal of Psychiatry*, **145**, 1232–1236.

Brogan, P. (1989). *World Conflicts. Why and Where they Happen*. London: Bloomsbury.

Carlstrom, A., Lundin, T. & Otto, U. (1990). Mental adjustment of Swedish UN soldiers in South Lebanon in 1988. *Stress Medicine*, **6**, 305–310.

Crocq, I. & Crocq, M. A. (1987). Trauma and personality in the causation of war neurosis. In Belenky, G. (Ed.), *Contemporary Studies in Combat Psychiatry*. New York: Greenwood Press.

Crocq, L., Sailhan, H. & Barrois, C. (1983). Neuroses traumatiques. In *Encyclopédie de Médicine et de Chirurgie*. Paris: Psychiatrie.

Crocq, M. A., Hein, K. D., Duval, F. & Macher, J. P. (1991). Severity of the prisoner of war experience and post-traumatic stress disorder. *European Psychiatry* **6**, 39–45.

Davidson, J. R. T., Kudler, H. S., Saunders, W. B. & Smith, R. D. (1990). Symptom and comorbidity patterns in World War 2 and Vietnam veterans with post-traumatic stress disorder. *Comprehensive Psychiatry*, **31**, 162–170.

De Groen, J. H. M., Op den Velde, W., van Duijn, H., Falger, P. R. I., Hovens, J. E. & Flos, M. F. R. (1990). Post-traumatic nightmares and timing of REM sleep. *Journal of Interdisciplinary Cycle Research*, **21**, 192–193.

De Loos, W. S. (1990*a*). Psychosomatic manifestations of chronic posttraumatic stress disorder. In M. E. Wolf & A. D. Mosnaim, (Eds), *Posttraumatic Stress Disorder: Etiology, Phenomenology and Treatment*. Washington, DC: American Psychiatric Press.

De Loos, W. S. (1990*b*). Blood pressure and cortisol in traumatic stress reactions. (Abstract) *The Netherlands Journal of Medicine*, **37**, A39.

Druley, K. A. & Pashko, S. (1988). Post traumatic stress disorder in World War II and Korean combat veterans with alcohol dependency. *Recent Developments in Alcoholism*, **6**, 89–101.

Eitinger, L. (1958). *Psykiatriske Undersøkelser Bland Flyktninger i Norge* (English summary). Oslo: Universitetsforlaget.

Eitinger, L. (1964). *Concentration Camp Survivors in Norway and Israel*. Oslo: Universitetsforlaget.

Eitinger, L. & Strøm, A. (1973). *Mortality and Morbidity after Excessive Stress*. Oslo: Universitetsforlaget.

Eitinger, L. & Strøm, A. (1981). New investigations on the mortality and morbidity of Norwegian ex-concentration camp prisoners. *Israel Journal of Psychiatry and Related Sciences*, **18**, 173–195.

Ellenberger, H. F. (1974). *A la Découverte de l'Inconscient*. Villeurbanne: Simep.

Emerson, G. (1976). *Winners and Losers. Battles, Retreats, Gains, Losses and Ruins from the Vietnam War*. Harmondsworth: Penguin.

Falger, P. R. J. (1989). Life span development and myocardial infarction: An epidemiological study. PhD thesis. Maastricht: University of Limburg School of Medicine.

Falger, P. R. J., Op den Velde, W., Hovens, J. E. & Schouten, E. G. W. (in press). Current post traumatic stress disorder and cardiovascular risk factors in Dutch resistance veterans from World War II. In W. S. De Loos & W. Op den Velde (Eds), *Selected Proceedings of Second European Conference on Traumatic Stress. Psychotherapy and Psychosomatics.*

Feinstein, A. & Dolan, R. (1991). Predictors of post traumatic stress disorder following physical trauma: An examination of the stressor criterion. *Psychological Medicine*, **21**, 85–91.

Figley, C. R. (1986). Traumatic stress: The role of the family and social support system. In C. R. Figley (Ed.), *Trauma and Its Wake*, vol. II. New York: Brunner Mazel.

Fischer-Homberger, E. (1975). *Die Traumatische Neurose*. Stuttgart: Huber.

Fraser, R., Leslie, I. M. & Phelps, D. (1942/43). Psychiatric effects of personal experience of bombing. *Proceedings of the Royal Society of Medicine*, **36**, 111–123.

Goldberg, D. P. (1978). *The Detection of Psychiatric Illness by Questionnaire*. London: Oxford University Press.

Green, B. L., Grace, M. C., Lindy, J. D. & Gleser, G. C. (1990). War stressors and symptom persistence in post-traumatic stress disorder. *Journal of Anxiety Disorders*, **4**, 31–39.

Hamilton, J. D. & Canteen, W. (1987). Posttraumatic stress disorder in World War II naval veterans. *Hospital and Community Psychiatry*, **38**, 197–199.

Helweg-Larsen, P., Hoffmeyer, H., Kieler, F., Hess-Thaysen, E., Thygesen, P. & Wulff, M. H. (1952). Famine disease in German concentration camps. *Acta Psychiatrica Scandinavica*, **83**, 17–21.

Höpker, W. W. (1982). *Spätfolgen Extremer Lebensverhältnisse*. Stuttgart: Gentner.

Horowitz, M. J. (1990). A model of mourning: Change in schemas of self and other. *Journal of the American Psychoanalytical Association*, **38**, 297–324.

Hovens, J. E., Op den Velde, W., Falger, P. R. J., Schouten, E. G. W., de Groen, J. H. M. & van Duijn, H. (in press). Anxiety, depression and anger in Dutch resistance veterans from World War II. In W. S. de Loos & W. Op den Velde (Eds), *Selected Proceedings of the Second European Conference on Traumatic Stress. Psychotherapy and Psychosomatics.*

Juillet, R. & Moutin, P. (1969). *Psychiatrie Militaire*. Paris: Masson.

Kammerer, T. (1967). Réflexion sur le traumatisme psychique. *Evolutions Psychiatriques*, **32**, 65–87.

Ketner, B. (1972). Combat strain and subsequent mental health. A follow-up study of Swedish soldiers serving in the United Nations forces 1961–62. *Acta Psychiatrica Scandinavica*, Supplement No. 230.

Lefebvre, P. (1982). La psychiatrie d'urgence en temps de guerre. *Rapport au Comité Consultatif de Santé des Armées*, Paris.

Lundin, T. & Otto, U. (1989). Stress reactions among Swedish health care personnel in UNIFIL, South Lebanon 1982–84. *Stress Medicine*, **5**, 237–246.

Lundin, T. & Otto, U. (in press). Swedish UN soldiers in Cyprus, UNFICYP: Their psychological and social situation. In De Loos, W. S. & Op den Velde, W. (Eds), *Selected Proceedings of Second European Conference on Traumatic Stress. Psychotherapy and Psychosomatics.*

Main, T. (1989). *The Ailment and Other Psychoanalytic Essays*. London: Free Association Books.

Marciniak, R. D. (1986). Implications to forensic psychiatry of posttraumatic stress disorder: A review. *Military Medicine*, **151**, 434–437.

Miller, T. W., Martin, W. & Spiro, K. (1989). Traumatic stress disorder: Diagnostic and clinical issues in former prisoners of war. *Comprehensive Psychiatry*, **30**, 139–149.

Myers, C. S. (1940). *Shell Shock in France, 1914–1918*. Cambridge: Cambridge University Press.

O'Brien, L. S. & Hughes, S. J. (1991). Symptoms of post-traumatic stress disorder in Falklands veterans five years after the conflict. *British Journal of Psychiatry*, **159**, 135–141.

Op den Velde, W. (1988). Specific psychiatric disorders. In J. F. P. Hers & J. Terpstra (Eds), *Stress, Medical and Legal Analysis of Late Effects of World War II Suffering in the Netherlands*. Alphen aan den Rijn: Samson Sijthoff.

Op den Velde, W., Falger, P. R. J., de Groen, J. H. M., van Duijn, H., Hovens, J. E., Meijer, P., Soons, M. & Schouten, E. G. W. (1990). Current psychiatric complaints of Dutch resistance veterans from World War II: A feasibility study. *Journal of Traumatic Stress*, **3**, 351–358.

Ørner, R. J. (in press). Post-traumatic stress syndromes among British veterans of the Falklands War.

In J. P. Wilson & B. Raphael (Eds), *The International Handbook of Traumatic Stress Syndromes*. New York: Plenum Press.

Paul, H. A. (1986). *Einflüsse Extremer Belastungen auf die Psychischen und Psychosocialen Verhältnisse Ehemaliger Kriegsgefangener*. Stuttgart: Gentner.

Ponteva, M. (1977). Psykiatriset sairaudet Suomen puolustusvoimissa v.v. 1941–1944. *Sotilaslääketieellinen Aikakauslehti*, **52**, 31–208.

Rosen, J. & Fields, R. (1988). The long term effects of extraordinary trauma: A look beyond PTSD. *Journal of Anxiety Disorders*, **2**, 179–191.

Schenck, E. G. (1975). *Katamnetische Erhebungen über Ehemalige Kriegsgefangene. Saarland Studie*. Stuttgart: Gentner.

Schenck, E. G. (1976). *Ergebnisse einer Befragung und Untersuchung Ehemaliger Kriegsgefangenen*. Stuttgart Studie. Stuttgart: Gentner.

Schenck, E. G. (1979). *Die Ärztliche Beurteilung von Gesundheitsschäden bei Ehemaligen Kriegsgefangenen*. Stuttgart: Gentner.

Schenck, E. G., Scheidt T. G. & Goetz, E. (1984). *Sterbearten und Todesursachen Ehemaliger Wehrmachtsangehöriger mit und ohne Kriegsgefangenschaft Sowie Rassisch und Politisch Verfolgter*. München Studie. Stuttgart: Gentner.

Shatan, C. F., Haley, S. & Smith, J. (1977). Johnny comes home: Combat stress and DSM-III. Paper presented at the American Psychiatric Association Annual Meeting, Toronto, May.

Showalter, E. (1987). *The Female Malady: Women, Madness and English Culture, 1830–1980*. London: Virago Press.

Sigg, B. W. (1989). *Le Silence et la Honte: Neuroses de la Guerre d'Algerie*. Paris: Messidor.

Sivard, R. L. (1987). *World Military and Social Expenditure 1987–88*, 12th ed. Washington DC: World Priorities.

Stern, H. (1918). Die hysterosomatischen Störungen als Massenerscheinung im Krieg (Therapie und Prognosis). *Zeitung für Gesundheit, Psychiatrie und Neurologie*, **38**, 61–69.

Stoering, G. (1942). *Medizinsche Woche*. January. Munich.

Stretch, R. H. (1986). Posttraumatic stress disorder among Vietnam and Vietnam era veterans. In C. R. Figley (Ed.), *Trauma and its Wake*, vol. II. New York: Brunner Mazel.

Sutter, J. (1986). Les neuroses traumatiques de guerre: Évolution des idées. *Psychiatrie Française*, **5**, 9–20.

Thürauf, J., Schenck, E. G., Valentin, H. & Weltle, D. (1975). *Studie über die Sterblichkeit Ehemaliger Kriegsgefangener in Nürnberg*. Nürnberg Studie. Stuttgart: Gentner.

Torrie, A. (1944). Psychosomatic casualties in the Middle East. *Lancet*, i, 139–143.

Trimble, M. R. (1985). Post traumatic stress disorders: History of a concept. In R. C. Figley (Ed.), *Trauma and its Wake*, vol. 1. New York: Brunner Mazel.

van den Dungen, P. (1981). Disablement and war. *Reconciliation Quarterly*, **3**, 23–29.

Weisaeth, L. (1990). Stress of peace keeping. In J. E. Lundberg, U. Otto & B. Rybeck (Eds), *Wartime Medical Services*. Stockholm: FOA.

Weisaeth, L. & Sund, A. (1982). Psychiatric problems in Unifil and the UN soldier's stress syndrome. *Revue International de Santé*, **55**, 109–116.

Wilson, J. P., Harel, Z. & Kahana, B. (1988). *Human Adaptation to Extreme Stress. From the Holocaust to Vietnam*. London: Plenum Press.

Yager, T., Laufer, R. & Gallops, M. (1984). Some problems associated with war experience in men of the Vietnam generation. *Archives of General Psychiatry*, **41**, 327–333.

British Journal of Clinical Psychology (1992), **31**, 405–417   *Printed in Great Britain*

Patterns of service for the long-term mentally ill in Europe

L. A. Rowland*

Department of Psychology, Institute of Psychiatry, De Crespigny Park, Denmark Hill, London SE5 8AF, UK

J. Zeelan

Institute of Andragology, State University of Groningen, Groningen, The Netherlands

L. C. Waismann

Instituto Andaluz de Salud Mental, Sevilla, Spain

Mental health services are organized and financed in very different ways across Europe; nevertheless there are a number of common trends and issues. In this paper we deal with some of those issues which influence the quality of services to those with long-term and severe mental health problems and disabilities. The most obvious trend has been the rundown of psychiatric beds particularly in the large mental hospitals and this in its turn has given rise to the problem of providing alternative services. Throughout Europe people are striving, with mixed success, to establish new services that are community orientated, provide reasonable levels of clinical care with some continuity and coordination, and ensure that the individuals served have appropriate accommodation and day-time activities. While there are some excellent services, there are even more services throughout Europe struggling to solve common problems. We have tried to draw some lessons from their efforts.

A number of publications have appeared in recent years seeking to provide an overview or to make comparisons between the mental health services of various European States (e.g. Bennett, 1991; Mangen, 1985, 1988; May, 1976; WHO, 1987). The task has not proved to be an easy one. Comparisons even at the level of supposedly 'hard data' such as the numbers of beds available or admission rates have proved difficult. Not only are the data collected in different countries not always comparable but there are discrepancies between even such fundamental terms as 'patient' and 'bed' (Bennett, 1991; Dupont, 1987). In part as a response to this situation the WHO initiated its comparative study of 21 mental health services in pilot study areas covering 16 countries.

The situation is even more complicated and the information less readily available

* Requests for reprints.

when we turn to the areas of social policy, service organization, finance and practice. 'Nevertheless, some comparisons can challenge current national assumptions and can add extra dimension to the perception of any country's problems, as well as providing clues for possible new approaches to their resolution' (Bennett, 1991, p. 626).

Perhaps the two most important factors in determining the development and delivery of services to people with long-term and severe mental health problems are the ways in which these services are financed and the ways in which they are planned (Mangen, 1985). These are large and complex issues beyond the scope of the present article. Our aim here is to attempt to identify some of the common themes in service delivery and practice. Issues such as the need to ensure continuity in the care of people with severe and long-term disabilities; the provision of community orientated services, as the large institutions are run down; the need for a range of accommodation and day-time activity in the provision of the comprehensive service; and the importance of identifying the population to be served. In addition to identifying these issues, we also provide brief examples of the ways in which various services around Europe have attempted to address them. The examples are sometimes of innovative solutions but equally often of what appears to be emerging as 'good practice'.

Continuity of care

There is an increasing appreciation of the importance of continuity of care, ensuring that people receive services when they need them (Barbato, Terzian, Saraceno, Barquero & Tognoni, 1992; Cooper, 1987; Mognolli, Faccincani & Platt, 1991; Steffansson, Cullberg & Steinholtz Ekecrantz, 1990; Tansella, 1991; ten Horn, 1984). Unfortunately as yet there is no generally accepted definition of continuity. Most commonly it is used in a chronological sense, but one can also have continuity of approach or philosophy, of location or of personnel.

(i) Continuing care

Continued responsibility is important, but if we look around Europe there are formidable obstacles to achieving it. In Holland, for example, ten Horn (1984) found that only 53 per cent of patients who needed aftercare received it. Of these, 18 per cent had only one out-patient contact. Giel & ten Horn (1982) and Schrameijer (1987) have concluded that the separate origins and autonomy of the agencies who ought to provide this element of care constitute a major obstacle to continuity of care.

In Germany (Cooper, 1987; Cooper & Bauer, 1987; Haerlin, 1987; Mangen, 1985) continuity of care has been hindered by the manner in which services are financed, and by the influential position held by private office practitioners and the health insurance schemes. Psychiatric hospitals have only recently been allowed to establish out-patient clinics and these have significant restrictions placed on them. 'Health insurance schemes do not cover the full treatment costs. This has hindered the development of the required multi-disciplinary team structures and has made hospital administration reluctant to instigate these "loss-making" services' (Haerlin, 1987, p. 196).

Despite these difficulties, in many of the better services they have been striving to find imaginative ways to provide continuity. For example, by 1987 30 out-patient clinics had been established (Haerlin, 1987), and in Bavaria a scheme has been developed which enables ex-patients attending the day centre to visit the hospital when they are 'well', enabling them to maintain contact with those who looked after them while they were 'ill'.

In Italy the guarantee of continuity of care varies substantially from region to region (Barbato *et al.*, 1992; Becker, 1985; Pirella, 1987; Tognoni & Saraceno, 1989). Barbato *et al.* looked at the number of patients who were still in contact with their local community psychiatric services six months after discharge from an in-patient admission in eight regions of Italy. Using this definition, continuity of care was deemed to have been achieved for 51 per cent of patients. The authors of this study hypothesized that lack of continuity for the remaining 49 per cent was the result either of 'inadequate integration between in-patient and community services, or inappropriate hospitalization' (p. 50).

In many rehabilitation units and hostels throughout Europe the ratio of staff to patients is in the order of 1:1 or 1:2. For 'follow-up', however, this typically declines to 1:15, 1:20 or 1:30. Many of those involved in 'aftercare' complain that it is all they can do to keep up with crises. As long as there is some part of the service designated as 'aftercare' there is the danger that it will be regarded as being after the 'main treatment and involvement'. Where this is the case both resources and energy can be concentrated on what is perceived as the important 'treatment phase'. Many people, however, need continuing care tailored to their needs.

(ii) Coherence and comprehensiveness

In Bern the emphasis is placed on continuity across the various areas of the individual's life rather than risk fragmenting his/her care. Thus, the hostel, the workshop and the therapeutic staff work as a single team. Decisions made in any one area are informed by and complement those in all others. Such an approach to continuity might be known as coherence. In the absence of this form of continuity, as 'a patient progresses through a series of service elements ... his/her use of the particular elements of that service is determined more by the nature of the services than by his/her characteristics as a patient' (Bennett, 1991, p. 268).

Perhaps the best-known example of an attempt to provide continuity of care is the service in Trieste, where they attempt to provide chronological continuity, coherence and comprehensiveness (Bennett, 1980, 1985; Dell'Acqua & Coglia Dezza, 1985; Giannichedda, 1987; Lovestone, 1986). The Mental Health Centres (MHC) provide the core of this service, each one serving a catchment area of 30000–45000. They provide a wide and flexible range of care from 24-hour care, through day or night care, to providing support for the individual in his/her own home. In addition, they have a psychiatric emergency clinic with eight beds and a range of supported accommodation.

The service in South Verona similarly strives to achieve these goals. It consists of: a Mental Health Centre providing day care and rehabilitation, a domiciliary service providing both emergency and elective care, an out-patient department, a 15-bed in-patient unit, and an emergency clinic service open 24 hours a day. In addition, temporary accommodation can be paid for and a cooperative provides both work and help with cooking, cleaning and shopping (Tansella, Balestrieri, Meneghelli & Micciolo, 1991). All staff except nurses (there are hospital, hostel and community nurses) work both inside and outside the hospital in an effort to ensure continuity of care.

How to achieve continuity, comprehensiveness and coherence has also been addressed in Germany following a major review of the mental health services. The 1975 Enquète (Cooper, 1987) recommended that 'Model Psychiatry Programmes' should be set up in various regions of the country. In the event such programmes were set up in 14 areas. Cooper's conclusion on these projects was: '[the] range of services promoted as part of the Model Psychiatric Programme indicates that the official policy of encouraging local and regional developments in this field of care achieved a measure of practical success. At the same time, it demonstrates the fragmented nature of these developments and hence the complexity of the situation which must be faced by anyone wishing to make a global assessment' (p. 102).

Many services throughout Europe have tackled the issue of ensuring continuity of care, but given the differences between nations in the organization of mental health care, no one, generally applicable, model has emerged. Most of the better services do, however, appear to be striving to achieve continuity over time, to coordinate the care of the individual and to identify his/her needs and in this way provide a comprehensive service.

Community care

It would be impossible to comment on what is happening in Europe without addressing the issue of community care. Like 'continuity', the term is used in a variety of ways: to describe policies and activities but most often, rather aridly, merely the reduction of hospital beds or the establishment of hostels. Tansella (1991) has commented that the word has lost its meaning and become a mere slogan.

(i) Non-hospital care

At times 'community care' seems to mean little more than 'not in hospital'. It is an expression of the sterile hospital vs. community debate. The fruitlessness of this debate is well illustrated by the organization of the services in Brussels and Kortenberg. Although most facilities are 'in the community', the initiative for service development came from hospital staff and the functions which the hospital fulfils are a pivotal feature of this service. One aspect of this service needs to be highlighted here, the Night Hospital in Brussels. This is a 44-place unit. Most patients have a diagnosis of schizophrenia and on average have been in contact with psychiatric services for more than 10 years. They are all involved in some form of day-time activity, 'in the community', during the day. In the evening they return to the night hospital, where they are expected to perform normal, individually tailored, domestic chores.

The patients in this service do not see the 'Night Hospital' as a hospital nor themselves as traditional patients. The emphasis is on being 'normal' during the day and on coping with their difficulties in the evenings. Nor do they perceive the 'Night Hospital' as just a large hostel. It offers more structure, is better staffed and, perhaps most importantly, offers asylum, support and intervention, allowing the patients to survive 'more normally' during the day (Pieters, 1987).

It would be fruitless to promote a debate about whether the Night Hospital is 'really' a hospital or 'really' a hostel, or whether it is 'really' community care or not. From the patients' point of view, it is a valuable service meeting their needs. It appears to be a beneficial use of resources to serve a wide range of functions.

In this context there are lessons to be learned from the studies conducted on the services in the Nacka-Värmdö project outside Stockholm (Stafansson & Cullberg, 1986; Stafansson *et al.*, 1990; Borga, Widerlov, Cullberg & Stafansson, 1991). Stafansson *et al.* (1990) describe the prevailing philosophy in Sweden as follows: 'The psychiatric care ideology … prevailing emphasized a psychiatric care organization that was easily accessible for people with mental health problems and that had responsibility for mental health care in defined catchment areas. It was based on out-patient care, a minimum of in-patient care and a multi-professional and varied treatment content' (p. 157).

In the Nacka-Värmdö sector a radical reorganization took place in 1975 moving from mainly institutional care with only two psychiatrists and one social worker providing out-patient care to a local 'community health organization' responsibility for all adult psychiatry care. Three multidisciplinary teams were set up and a 24-hour emergency service was offered. Treatment was mainly 'psychodynamic and social psychiatry' and pharmacotherapy was used where appropriate (Stafansson & Cullberg, 1986). After a two-year follow-up period Stafansson & Cullberg concluded that the new service provided more care but that patients were now 'relatively less disturbed psychiatrically, and a larger proportion had not received psychiatric treatment previously'.

The closure of the local mental hospital led to a substantial reorganization of the service (Stafansson *et al.*, 1990). More of the local resources were dedicated to 'specialized out-patient care' for the long-term psychiatrically ill patients. Consultation without appointment was cut back, emergencies were directed either to primary care or to the emergency department of the hospital. The sector assumed responsibility for 58 beds so that long-term patients could be cared for within the organization. Out-patient care was also reorganized with one of the three clinics devoted to individuals with long-term psychotic problems. The conclusion of this study was that 'easily accessible' services do not necessarily provide the ideal service organization for people with long-term and severe mental health problems and disabilities. One has to consider the type and organization of services and identify a target population, determining the best method of service delivery.

Tansella's (1991) definition of community care or rather 'community based psychiatry' picks up on several of these themes: it is 'a system of care devoted to a defined population and based on a comprehensive and integrated mental health service. Such a service should include a wide spectrum of outpatient, day patient and general hospital inpatient facilities as well as staffed and unstaffed residential facilities. It should ensure multi-disciplinary team work, early diagnosis, prompt treatment, continuity of care, social support and close liaison with other community medical and social services, in particular GPs. According to this definition the mental hospital is intended to be gradually superseded and finally closed' (p. 47).

One of the largest and most energetic non-hospital schemes must be that run by the Sopimusvuori Society in Finland. From small beginnings, a hostel for six long-stay women patients, has grown up a range of different sorts of accommodation (ca 145 places), day centres (ca 120 places), and sheltered work (ca 120 places) for a catchment area of ca 330 000. Even this society was founded by a nurse and the initial project was supported by the hospital. Since 1972, however, it has been a vigorous and independent 'private' society (voluntary organization), to which the planning and provision of local facilities for individuals with long-term disabilities has been largely subcontracted (Ojanen, 1984).

The extreme in care by the community is to be found in Geel, Belgium. Geel's extant records date back to the 15th century. Patients, usually long-stay patients, come from all over Flemish-speaking Belgium, to a lesser extent from French-speaking Belgium and from abroad, and are placed with a foster family in Geel. Each patient's progress is followed by a nurse who visits on a regular basis and sees the patient once a fortnight away from the family environment. The project has its own in-patient unit.

In a series of 64 consecutive admissions it was found that: 54 patients either returned to their natural families or were well integrated in the programme and out of hospital. At least to the extent that it keeps people out of hospital the programme appears to be successful. Srole, an American social anthropologist involved in a study of the Geel project, felt that the benefits are greater than this: '(1) they (the foster family patients) were actively engaged in the business of normal family living, rather than apathetically disengaged, and (2) outer-directed in their public-behaviours, rather than inaccessibly withdrawn into their private world' (Srole, 1976, p. 9).

The rate of referrals to this programme has declined in recent years as the long-stay patient population in Belgium has declined and a variety of initiatives in other parts of the country have got under way. Whether or not Geel survives it might prove profitable to identify why some individuals, unacceptable in their own families, have survived in the foster family situation. It seems likely that the philosophy of the programme will reduce some of the more pathogenic elements sometimes found in families. The general approach in Geel is one of tolerance and acceptance, and the foster family's job is not to act as therapists. This must reduce the dangers of such precipitants of disturbed behaviour and relapse as high expressed emotion, especially overinvolvement. The programme also suggests that the skills of the lay person in resocializing, stimulating and supporting the patients are often underestimated. The programme has appreciated that the foster families need backup, and that the patients need both day-time activity and the possibility of privacy—a room of their own.

(ii) Targetting the population

The importance of targetting those individuals with severe and long-term disabilities has already been identified. Many authors have, however, expressed their concern about the care that may be provided for this most disabled group. In Germany, for example, Cooper (1987) has commented that the way in which the health insurance schemes work 'makes it difficult for them to do justice to the needs for long-term care and rehabilitation of the long-term mentally ill and handicapped' (p. 99).

Eikelmann & Reker (1991), again in Germany, have commented that while more interest is being shown in the extramural care of the chronically mentally ill the emphasis tends to be on residential rehabilitation. 'They often fail to take account of the fact that extramural care of the chronically ill patient has to do justice on a multi-dimensional plane to numerous medical, psychological and social needs' (p. 357).

More outspokenly, Goldie & Freden (1991), commenting on Swedish psychiatry, have said: 'The "new psychiatry" has been paid for by the schizophrenic patients. Resources used to build up this new psychiatry and also psychotherapy have been paid for by the decline in beds of schizophrenic patients. Resources formally used for schizophrenic inpatients are not now being used for them as outpatients' (p. 503).

Perhaps the most damning statement comes from Mangen (1988) in his overview of services internationally: 'The major conclusion is that, whatever the system of health care, it has been the long-term mentally ill who have been deprived of adequate resources and who continue to be in receipt of "Cinderella" services' (p. 27).

Accommodation

Probably the greatest single consequence of the rundown of hospital beds has been the explosion of 'non-hospital' accommodation. While some may have been slow to appreciate the importance of day care almost everyone appreciates the need to have somewhere to lay one's head. The array of facilities is bewildering. One can find therapeutic communities, group homes, apartments housing people of mixed abilities and hostels with facilities for respite or crisis care. They are owned by health authorities, local government, voluntary organizations and private landlords.

The most common model throughout Europe is the 'group home' which offers accommodation to those with moderate levels of disabilities, who can perform their share of communal tasks and engage in day-time activities. It is unclear why this type of accommodation is so popular. It is certainly economical (cheap). Some claim that patients prefer this style of living because the alternative is loneliness, although few data have been produced to support this. Given this argument it is unclear why people are seen as suitable to move on and live alone primarily on the basis of their functional skills rather than on the basis of their social skills or the extent of their social network.

In a few places, for example in the hospital hostels in England (Young, 1991), they carry out assessment to identify the individual's needs and then construct appropriate programmes. The line between organizing resources to meet the needs of the individual and organizing the individual to sustain the institution can be a fine one. Kunze (1985) provides an example of what can happen when individualized assessment and programme planning does not take place. Following up 961 chronic psychiatric patients, he found that twice as many of them were in non-hospital accommodation as were in hospital. He also looked at the quality of care and social milieux in these community residences and found that in general the most disabled patients were in accommodation with the poorest social environment. He concluded that at least in the area of Germany he was looking at, 'for most chronic psychiatric patients the move from hospital to residential care outside the hospital system only meant transfer from one institutional situation to another' (p. 262).

With this in mind, it is important that the functions of planning patient care and ensuring financial viability are separated, and a system is found which ensures that the interests of the individual are not subordinated to those of the institution. It would also help if the minimum statutory requirements for residential accommodation for (ex-) psychiatric patients covered standards of care as well as the physical aspects of the accommodation.

A major reform of the psychiatric services in Andalucia, Spain, has been taking place in recent years. A network of integrated services is being developed and accommodation is playing an important role in these new structures, particularly in Malaga. Therapeutic communities have been established. These accommodate younger, more floridly disturbed individuals. Recently, a hostel for former long-stay patients was also established. Initially it was staffed 24 hours a day. At the end of a year most of the residents were found to have improved significantly, but the former hospital staff had difficulty in changing their attitudes. As a result, the house was substantially reorganized and nurses were replaced by non-health service personnel such as a cook, a cleaner, and care assistants, whose job it was to run the house and to befriend the residents. The result of this was that a more 'normal' atmosphere reigned. With a more flexible organization in place the needs of individual residents could be more easily addressed, rules could be changed and residents could be given greater autonomy. The hostel staff provided care and support and the community health team provided the health care. In addition to these clinical benefits, costs were also significantly reduced.

There is always the danger with accommodation projects that they are poorly integrated into the local community. Residents are cut off from many of their traditional support systems without new ones being developed. One way of avoiding this isolation is exemplified by the Hestia Housing Association in Tienen, Belgium. Besides having representatives of the health service on its management committee, ensuring that residents receive continued mental health care and are engaged in some form of day activity, the association has made available space for people from different houses to meet socially and eat together in the evenings when they want to. This is an idea mid-way between a common room, a club, a drop-in centre and the core in the core and cluster model of housing.

Another approach to avoiding some of these common pitfalls is exemplified by a hostel in Augsberg, Germany, which has 32 places. The danger is that a hostel of this size becomes a mini-institution. The staff have tackled this problem and attempted to use the size of the hostel to the residents' advantage. Residents are divided into living groups of four people, so all tasks are on a domestic scale. Given the size of the hostel, however, they have been able to organize a range of activities: a bicycle repair shop, woodwork, an art studio, a clerical office, and a sheltered work scheme. The resident's involvement in these activities is planned so as to meet his/her needs and at the same time to be consonant with other expectations placed on him/her.

Day care and vocational rehabilitation

Day care in a variety of forms is playing an increasingly important role in most European countries. However, although day care already has a significant history (e.g. Bennett, 1969; Luber, 1979) and its effectiveness has been reviewed (e.g. Schene & Gersons, 1986; Linn, Caffey, Klett, Hogarty & Lamb, 1979), the function of day care, whom it should be aimed at, where it fits into the system and what one does in day care seem as unclear as ever (e.g. Astrachan, Hulda, Geller & Harvey, 1970; Luber, 1979; Rowland, 1988; Schene & Gersons, 1986).

To illustrate this, Schene & Gersons (1986) found that only 9 per cent of patients in day care in the Netherlands were there as an alternative to in-patient treatment, and Steinhart & Bosch (1983), in West Germany, found that most referrals to day care came after hospitalization, though it was seen as an alternative to hospitalization. As already reported, in the Nacka-Värmdö project they had to radically restructure their services to ensure that the severely disabled were adequately served, but, in contrast, in Italy, for example in South Verona, the mental health centres provide a wide range of facilities for a varied clientele.

It would be easy to conclude that a lack of clarity as to the purpose of day care leads to a stereotyped service being offered. This would be too harsh. Different service models appear to result in the need for different types of day care. In the better services the day care tends to be well integrated, have a clear place in the overall service and clearly targets an identified population.

One form of day activity which is growing in importance throughout Europe is work. Work has long had a role in mental health services and its potential benefits have frequently been rehearsed (e.g. Bennett, 1975; Jahoda, 1985; Rowland & Perkins, 1988; Van Weeghel & Zeelan, 1990, 1992). Interest in this form of day activity is being renewed from European Community level, as it supports various initiatives through its Social Fund, down to the 'grass roots' level where there is a wide range of initiatives from the traditional industrial therapy units, to social firms, cooperatives and work placement schemes.

(*a*) Cooperatives and social firms have now been set up in Italy, Germany, the Netherlands, the United Kingdom and Spain. These are small businesses aimed at offering paid employment to people who, although able to contribute to a work situation, would be unable to cope with the strains of open employment. The preference often is for people with psychiatric problems to work together with people who have other problems. Often key positions in the production process are held by non-disabled employees. The psychiatrically disabled employees engage in appropriate production tasks, the non-disabled employees largely supervise and coordinate. In periods of relapse, the worker can move to a less complex, less stressful activity. The psychiatrically disabled workers are not considered as patients, but are employees with all the rights and duties that come with that position. The work done by the social firms and cooperatives is varied: small-scale agricultural businesses, restaurants, hotels, car washes, toy manufacturers, industrial workshops and shops.

(*b*) In the USA, UK, the Netherlands and Sweden clubhouses and day-activity centres have recently been developed which, besides their socializing function, also fulfil an important role in vocational rehabilitation. A well-known example is the Fountain House model which has been copied in a number of places in Europe (e.g. in Amsterdam). Fountain Houses are clubhouses for people with a psychiatric background (Beard, Propst & Malamud, 1982). Strong emphasis is put on a sense of belonging and the need to work together. Members are expected to help run the clubhouse. They carry out activities, from kitchen work to administration, from cleaning to editing the daily clubhouse newspaper. Each member, despite his psychiatric disability, is looked upon as a potential worker who can make a contribution according to his abilities and who can count on the appreciation and support of other members and staff.

In the Fountain House model return to regular employment is considered an essential aim of the rehabilitation process. By performing unpaid work within the clubhouse, members are expected to progress to paid work. In this way the internal 'pre-vocation day programme' is intended to prepare members for the Transitional Employment Programme (TEP). This is organized as follows: The Fountain House is in contact with various firms who agree to reserve a fixed number of jobs for clubhouse members. The Fountain House guarantees continuous occupation of these positions, which can be filled by different clubhouse members in turn. In this way the TEP offers clubhouse members the opportunity to gain experience in the open labour market, knowing that these jobs have already been tried by staff and/or other members and that the firms concerned are accustomed to employees with a psychiatric background.

(*c*) A third development is to be found mainly in Germany. Over the last few years a number of regions have established special outreach services to encourage the integration of people with psychiatric problems into the open labour market. These so-called 'psychosocial services' (PSS) offer support to clients who suffer difficulties in the work sphere. Many are threatened by dismissal, others are in danger of losing their jobs in the longer term because of difficulties related to their disabilities. A third group of PSS clients consists of people wishing to return to work after a long period in hospital or long-term treatment and who need intensive support. The service offers these clients a contact person who supports them intensively and, if necessary, continuously. These services often start up groups where clients can discuss the problems they experience at work. In addition, they provide advice and support to colleagues, supervisors and personnel managers and sometimes set up public courses.

Having reviewed the work provisions available Van Weeghel & Zeelan (1992) conclude that a range of work programmes are needed including: preparation programmes, transition programmes, sheltered work projects and support in open employment. However, a number of problems are commonly encountered in establishing and running work and vocational rehabilitation projects. Economic, political and cultural hindrances can all obstruct people with mental health problems and disabilities reintegrating into the employment market. There is wide-spread prejudice and discrimination. Legislation is more often targetted at those with physical disabilities than those with psychiatric disabilities. Establishing a sound economic basis for projects is often a major problem for social firms and cooperatives. Subsidies, which in most cases are needed on a long-term basis, may be withdrawn resulting in a tension between production demands and rehabilitation goals.

Conclusion

Despite differences in the way mental health services are financed and organized across Europe, there are a number of issues and themes common to most countries. Besides those that have been discussed, one might identify the trend towards sectorized services, the establishment of case registers for service evaluation and planning, assessment and the identification of needs, the importance and involvement of families, the users' movement, and many others which fall beyond the scope of the present article.

Given the diversity of services across Europe, one is drawn to the conclusion that there is no one model of service delivery which is universally applicable. Rather it would seem that good services are responsive to local conditions with the result that there will be a great deal of variation not only between but also within countries (Bachrach, 1982; Cooper, 1987). As we have attempted to illustrate, however, some themes do appear with some consistency, themes such as the need for continuity and coherence in the delivery of services, the need for the various elements of services to be well integrated, the need for a range of appropriate accommodation and day-time activities and the importance of targetting identified populations. There also appears to be a movement towards a consensus on some of these issues as to what might constitute good practice.

As Bennett (1991) has said, looking at the services of other countries can, at least, provide some clues to possible solutions to common problems. The challenge is in abstracting the principles from the ways in which they are realized in particular situations and then deciding how these same principles can be beneficially applied in one's own local situation.

The German 'Psychiatric-Enquete' recommended that the psychiatrically ill should have equal status with the physically ill and that community-based systems of care should be developed which are comprehensive and equitable for all psychiatric patients (Haerlin, 1987). The basic principles appear to be generally accepted throughout Europe today and underpin current attempts to develop services.

Acknowledgements

L.A.R. would like to thank Davina Kirby for her help in typing and editing and to Dr A. Conning for her comments on the original draft.

References

Astrachan, B. M., Hulda, R. F., Geller, J. D. & Harvey, H. H. (1970). Systems approach to day hospitalization. *Archives of General Psychiatry*, **22**, 550–559.

Bachrach, L. (1982). Assessment of outcomes in community support systems: Results, problems and limitations. *Schizophrenia Bulletin*, **8**, 39–60.

Barbato, A., Terzian, E., Saraceno, B., Barquero, F. M. & Tognoni, G. (1992). Patterns of aftercare for psychiatric patients discharged after short in-patient treatment. *Social Psychiatry and Psychiatric Epidemiology*, **27**, 46–52.

Beard, J. H., Propst, R. & Malamud, T. J. (1982). The Fountain House model of psychiatric rehabilitation. *Psychosocial Rehabilitation Journal*, Jan, pp. 47–53.

Becker, T. (1985). Psychiatric reform in Italy—How does it work in Piedmont? *British Journal of Psychiatry*, **147**, 254–260.

Bennett, D. H. (1969). The day hospital. *Bibliography of Psychiatry and Neurology*, **142**, 4–18.

Bennett, D. H. (1975). Techniques of industrial therapy: Ergotherapy and recreative methods. In Z. Auflange (Ed.), *Psychiatrie der Gegenwart*, vol. 3. Berlin: Springer-Verlag.

Bennett, D. H. (1980). An Italian model: Trieste. In *Changing Patterns in Mental Health Care*. Report on WHO Working Group (1978) Euro Reports and Studies No. 25. Copenhagen: WHO Regional Office, Europe.

Bennett, D. H. (1985). The changing pattern of mental health care in Trieste. *International Journal of Mental Health*, **14**, 70–92.

Bennett, D. H. (1991). The international perspective. In D. H. Bennett & H. L. Freeman (Eds), *Community Psychiatry: The Principles*. Edinburgh/London: Churchill Livingstone.

Borga, G., Widerlov, B., Cullberg, J. & Stafansson, C. J. (1991). Patterns of care among people with long-term functional psychosis in 3 different areas of Stockholm county. *Acta Psychiatrica Scandinavica*, **83**, 223–233.

Cooper, B. (1987). Mental health care models and their evaluation: The West German experience. *International Journal of Social Psychiatry*, **33**, 99–104.

Cooper, B. & Bauer, M. (1987). Developments in mental health care and services in the Federal Republic of Germany. *International Journal of Mental Health*, **16**, 78–92.

Dell'Acqua, G. & Coglia Dezza, M. G. (1985). The end of mental hospital. A review of the psychiatric experience in Trieste. *Acta Psychiatrica Scandinavica*, **316** (supplement), 45–69.

Dupont, A. (1987). Mental health information systems. In *Mental Health Services in Pilot Study Areas*. Copenhagen: World Health Organization.

Eikelmann, B. & Reker, T. (1991). A modern therapeutic approach for chronically mentally ill patients—Results of a four-year prospective study. *Acta Psychiatrica Scandinavica*, **84**, 357–363.

Enquète (1975). Bericht der Sachverständigen Kommission über die Lage det Psychiatrie in der Bundesrepublik Deutschland – Zur psychiatrischen und psychotherapeutisch/psychosomatischen Versorgung der Bevölkerung. Bonn: Drucksache 7/4200.

Giannichedda, M. G. (1987). Trieste, Italy. In *Mental Health Services in Pilot Study Areas*. Copenhagen: World Health Organization.

Giel, R. & ten Horn, G. H. M. M. (1982). Patterns of mental health care in a Dutch register area. *Social Psychiatry*, **17**, 117–123.

Goldie, N. & Freden, L. (1991). A 'crisis' of closure and openness: The present state of the Swedish mental health system in the light of a policy of sectorisation. *Social Science and Medicine*, **32**, 499–506.

Haerlin, C. (1987). Community care in West Germany: Concept and reality. *International Journal of Social Psychiatry*, **33**, 105–110.

Jahoda, M. (1985). Die sozialpsychologische Bedeutung von Arbeit. In D. Kleiber *et al.* (Eds), *Im Schatten der Wende*. Tübingen.

Kunze, H. (1985). Institutionalization in community care in West Germany. *British Journal of Psychiatry*, **147**, 261–264.

Linn, M. E., Caffey, E. M., Klett, C. J., Hogarty, G. E. & Lamb, H. R. (1979). Day treatment and psychotropic drugs in the aftercare of the schizophrenic patient. *Archives of General Psychiatry*, **36**, 1055–1066.

Lovestone, S. (1986). The Trieste experience. *Lancet*, **ii**, 1025–1028.

Luber, R. (1979). *Partial Hospitalization: A Current Perspective*. New York: Plenum Press.

Mangen, S. P. (1985). *Mental Health Care in the European Community*. London: Croom Helm.

Mangen, S. P. (1988). Implementing community care: An international assessment. In A. Lavender & F. Holloway (Eds), *Community Care in Practice*. Chichester: Wiley.

May, A. R. (1976). *Mental Health Services in Europe*. WHO offset publication: no. 23. Geneva: World Health Organization.

Mognolli, G., Faccincani, C. & Platt, S. (1991). Psychopathology and social performance in a cohort of patients with schizophrenic psychosis. A 7-year follow up study. *Psychological Medicine Monograph Supplement*, **19**, 17–26.

Ojanen, M. (1984). The Sopimusvuori Society: An integrated system of rehabilitation. *International Journal of Therapeutic Communities*, **5**, 193–208.

Pieters, G. (1987). The Brussels Night Hospital. In H. R. Dent (Ed.), *Clinical Psychology: Research and Development*. Beckenham: Croom Helm.

Pirella, A. (1987). The implementation of the Italian psychiatric reform in a large conurbation. *International Journal of Social Psychiatry*, **33**, 119–131.

Rowland, L. A. (1988). Dagaktiviteiten in een Europees Perspepektief. In *Dagakiviteiten voor (ex-) Psychiatrishe Patienten*. Gent: Nationale Vereniging voor Geestelijke Gezonheidszors v.z.w.

Rowland, L. A. & Perkins, R. E. (1988). You can't eat, drink or make love eight hours a day: The value of work in psychiatry—A personal view. *Health Trends*, **20**, 75–79.

Schene, A. H. & Gersons, B. P. R. (1986). Effectiveness and application of partial hospitalization. *Acta Psychiatrica Scandinavica*, **74**, 335–340.

Schrameijer, F. (1987). New comprehensive mental health authorities in the Netherlands. *International Journal of Social Psychiatry*, **33**, 132–136.

Srole, L. (1976). Geel (Belgium): The Natural Therapeutic Community, 1775–1975. Paper presented at the 4th International Symposium of Kittay Scientific Foundation.

Stafansson, C. G. & Cullberg, J. (1986). Introducing community mental health services. *Acta Psychiatrica Scandinavica*, **74**, 368–378.

Stafansson, C. G., Cullberg, J. & Steinholtz Ekecrantz, L. (1990). From Community Mental Health Services to specialized psychiatry: The effects of a change in policy on patient accessibility and care utilization. *Acta Psychiatrica Scandinavica*, **82**, 157–164.

Steinhart, I. & Bosch, G. (1983). Development and current status of partial hospitalization in the Federal Republic of Germany and West Berlin. *International Journal of Partial Hospitalization*, **2**, 71–81.

Tansella, M. (1991). Community care without mental hospitals: Ten years experience. *Psychological Medicine Monograph Supplement*, **19**, 47–54.

Tansella, M., Balestrieri, M., Meneghelli, G. & Micciolo, R. (1991). Trends in the provision of psychiatric care 1979–1988. *Psychological Medicine Monograph Supplement*, **19**, 5–16.

ten Horn, G. H. M. M. (1984). Aftercare and re-admission: A Dutch psychiatric case register study. *Social Psychiatry*, **19**, 111–116.

Tognoni, G. & Saraceno, B. (1989). Regional analysis and implementation. *International Journal of Social Psychiatry*, **35**, 38–45.

Van Weeghel, J. & Zeelan, J. (1990). *Arbeidsrehabilitatie in een vernieuwde geestelijke gezondheidszorg.* Utrecht: Lemma.

Van Weeghel, J. & Zeelan, J. (1992). Vocational rehabilitation in a changing psychiatry. Manuscript submitted for publication.

WHO (1987). *Mental Health Services in Pilot Study Areas.* Report on a European Study. Copenhagen: World Health Organization.

Young, R. (Ed.) (1991). *Residential Needs for Severely Disabled Psychiatric Patients: The Case for Hospital Hostels.* London: HMSO.

British Journal of Clinical Psychology (1992), **31**, 419–428 *Printed in Great Britain*

Clinical psychology training in Europe

Frank M. McPherson*

*Tayside Area Clinical Psychology Department, Royal Dundee Liff Hospital,
Dundee DD2 5NF, Scotland, UK*

Clinical psychology training in the United Kingdom (UK) and in the remainder of
Europe differs in several respects; in particular, the latter allows for greater
variability and clinical specialization with much more training taking place
postqualification than in the UK; differences in content and in the balance between
the supply of, and demand for, clinical psychologists also exist. These differences
reflect employment arrangements and, to a lesser extent, the structure of higher
education and legal regulation. Various current and predicted changes in health-care
systems and in the legal and educational context will probably lead to training in the
UK and elsewhere in Europe becoming more similar in the years after 1992.

The aims of this article are to describe some of the main similarities and differences
between clinical psychology training in the UK and in the rest of Europe, to consider
how training has been affected by its educational, employment and legal context, and
to identify some possible future influences on training.

There have been no systematic surveys of clinical psychology training in Europe.
The data on which this article is based are therefore: statements of training standards
and accreditation criteria produced by national associations of professional
psychology; descriptions of training programmes at various centres; evidence
presented to a task force of the European Federation of Professional Psychologists
Associations (EFPPA); documents of the World Health Organization, Council of
Europe and the European Community; published articles; and personal communications to, and (uncontrolled) observations by, the author.

Three limitations to this article should be noted. Firstly, the effects on clinical
psychology in Eastern Europe of the current social and political upheavals merit
separate consideration; the 'Europe' referred to in the article will thus include only
the Western European and Nordic States.

Secondly, it is not intended to describe in detail the content of training in the
different States. Such catalogues are soon out of date and are also potentially
misleading, in the absence of agreed definitions of terms such as 'supervised
experience' and 'year of study' and of an international system of on-site inspection
and peer review to ensure that what is described in each syllabus is reflected in
practice. Instead, some generalizations will be attempted. Inevitably, these will
ignore many of the significant differences which exist in clinical psychology training,
not only between, but often also within, the various European States.

---

* Requests for reprints.

Thirdly, the article will be written from a UK perspective and many of the contrasts and comparisons drawn will be between the UK and the remainder of Europe. This is only partly attributable to the narrow concerns and interests of the author; it also reflects his judgement that greater variation in training and practice exists between the UK and Continental Europe than exists within most of the latter.

The context of training

This section will outline the main features of the educational, employment and legal context within which clinical psychology training takes place.

Structure of higher education

The structure of higher education in the UK and Ireland (and in the USA) distinguishes between three phases: undergraduate, postgraduate and post-qualification (undergraduate, graduate and postgraduate in US parlance). The first (undergraduate) degree course in psychology is construed as an education in the scientific discipline, whereas the training necessary to become qualified as a clinical psychologist is exclusively the concern of the second (postgraduate) phase.

Elsewhere in Europe, these undergraduate and postgraduate phases are usually combined and the potential clinical psychologist embarks on a single degree course, at the completion of which s/he is regarded as a qualified professional psychologist. Usually, the early semesters are devoted to the basic science of psychology while, in the latter years, some measure of specialization occurs, with students able to choose subjects relevant to either 'academic/research' or 'professional applied' psychology.

Employment of clinical psychologists

For the past 45 years, the National Health Service (NHS) has been much the largest employer of clinical psychologists in the UK. The clinical policies, organizational and managerial arrangements, professional norms, entry requirements and conditions of employment of the NHS have been the major influence on the profession (McPherson, 1983 *a*, *b*).

Elsewhere in Europe, by contrast, the employment arrangements are very much more diverse. A higher proportion of clinical psychologists are in independent, fee-for-service practice. Those who are salaried have a much wider range of employers, such as State agencies, regional and municipal authorities, private hospitals and institutions and charities.

Legal regulation

Several European States have no form of legal regulation; these include some with well-developed professions of clinical psychology, e.g. the former German Federal Republic (BRD), Denmark, Ireland, Finland and Belgium. Where regulation does exist, the usual form is a certification law, which protects the title obtained on completion of the university degree. Laws of this type exist in Spain, Portugal, Italy,

France, Austria, Norway, Iceland and The Netherlands. In addition, some States have licensing laws which regulate the practice of clinical psychology and/or of psychotherapy, e.g. Austria, Italy, The Netherlands and Sweden (McPherson, 1986).

In most States, professional regulation is the responsibility of a Government department and there are big variations in the influence of the profession upon the content and administration of any laws. Spain and the UK are unusual in that the national association of psychologists has been given legal authority by the State to regulate qualifications and practice, although the powers of the Colegio are much greater than those of the British Psychological Society (BPS).

Similarities and differences in training

This section will identify similarities and differences in training which exist, in particular between the UK and elsewhere in Europe.

Length of training to qualification

In the UK, the minimum period of education and training necessary for registration with the BPS as a chartered clinical psychologist and, from 1993, for employment in the NHS is six years – three undergraduate and three postgraduate years.

This is roughly similar to the minimum periods of study and training in Europe, at the end of which graduates are regarded as qualified professional psychologists: e.g. approximately five years in Spain, Sweden and Denmark; six years in Italy, the BRD and Finland; and six and a half years in Norway.

As noted above, comparisons are difficult. The implications for training of a 'year of study' vary considerably because of differences in the numbers of contact hours within the year and in the form of teaching. Moreover, in the UK, many potential clinical psychologists spend several years obtaining relevant experience before being selected for training. In most of Europe, students enjoy some freedom to determine when to take their exams, so that the actual period of study and training is often two or more years longer than the minimum prescribed.

Basic science preparation

Clinical training throughout Europe seems always to be preceded by the systematic study of the scientific discipline of psychology. In the UK, this is the role of the undergraduate phase; elsewhere the first semesters of the single degree are usually devoted to basic science subjects. There is a wide measure of agreement about the topics which should be included in this basic science component. EFPPA recently formulated a set of 'optimal standards' for the training of professional psychologists (EFPPA, 1990). The list of 'core' topics was very similar to that recommended by various US organizations concerned with training (Matarazzo, 1987) and included: research design, statistics and measurement; scientific and professional ethics; the biological, cognitive–affective and social bases of behaviour; and individual differences. Of course, within these broad topic categories, there may well be significant differences in what is taught and to what level.

Supervised experience at the prequalification phase

Compared with their UK counterparts, potential clinical psychologists elsewhere in Europe usually obtain relatively little supervised clinical experience prior to qualification. A chartered clinical psychologist in the UK will have spent at least 18 months of direct clinical work, with mandatory placements with adults, children and adolescents, people with learning difficulties (mental handicap) and the elderly. Elsewhere, much shorter periods are necessary. For example, Norway requires *practicum* periods totalling eight months, the BRD and Denmark six months, while in The Netherlands it is possible to become a State-registered professional psychologist having had no placement experience.

A major reason for this difference is that, until recently in much of Europe, the concept 'postgraduate student', i.e. a graduate who returns to university to receive advanced training through formal supervision, was relatively unknown (Blume, 1988). Universities have therefore tended to see their role as that of providing the educational preparation for professional psychology, with most of the necessary practical experience being obtained after qualification. UK universities, on the other hand, have traditionally been closely involved in the practical training of many professions.

Role of postqualification training

There are thus major differences between the UK and elsewhere in the role of the postqualification phase of training. In the UK, it is relatively unimportant and, once a clinical psychologist is deemed to be qualified, there is no requirement for him/her to obtain further training. The few postqualification courses which are organized by the BPS and other bodies are usually short, *ad hoc* and have no formal implications for employment or professional standing.

Elsewhere, postqualification training has a major role, both in compensating for deficiencies in prequalification practical experience and in providing advanced training in particular specialisms, clinical areas or techniques. A very high proportion of clinical psychologists undertake formal training at this phase. In some States, e.g. Norway, it is necessary to have done an advanced 'specialist' training to be eligible for appointment to certain senior clinical posts in the health-care system. In others, e.g. Italy, Sweden and Austria, it is necessary to obtain systematic postqualification training in order legally to practise psychotherapy. In the BRD, health insurance companies will reimburse the fees of clinical psychologists who engage in psychoanalytic or behavioural psychotherapy only if they have attended approved practical and theoretical courses.

Postqualification training is often long and extensive. For example, Norway requires the qualified psychologist to have spent two years of supervised practice before starting on the 'specialist' training of at least five years, covering course work, supervised clinical practice and varied experience within the area of specialization. The Finnish specialization studies take four years part-time and include course work, supervised experience and a research dissertation or articles.

Common as opposed to individualized training

Compared with the UK, clinical training elsewhere in Europe is usually much less prescribed and uniform. Traditionally, students have had greater freedom to devise their own programme of academic studies. This choice often also extends to any practical placements undertaken, although these must usually satisfy criteria relating to the amount of supervision and client contact. There is no equivalent of the detailed specification by the BPS of the academic content, practical training and supervised experience of UK training courses.

Generic and specialized training

A related issue is the extent to which the training of clinical psychologists is 'generic' as opposed to specialized.

Professional applied psychology. In most European universities, during the later semesters of their single degree programme, students are often required to attend courses relevant not only to clinical psychology but also to at least one of the other branches of professional applied psychology, such as educational or occupational psychology. By contrast, UK undergraduate courses usually provide little or no experience of professional practice and postgraduate (prequalification) courses provide training exclusively in clinical, educational or occupational psychology.

Partly, this difference reflects the Continental European view that the degree is an educational preparation for, rather than a specific training in, professional practice. However, another factor in the UK is the close identification of each branch of professional applied psychology with specific employers, e.g. clinical psychology with the NHS and educational psychology with local authorities. These employers fund most of the prequalification training for their specific branch; moreover, their employment arrangements are such as to discourage psychologists from transferring from one branch to another. Clinical psychologists in the UK will thus usually have had little or no exposure to educational or occupational psychology; in this sense, UK training is less 'generic' than in most European States.

Clinical psychology. However, *clinical* psychology training in the UK is probably more 'generic', in that courses are explicitly intended to provide trainees with extensive experience of a range of client groups, clinical models and therapeutic and assessment approaches, in a variety of settings. Elsewhere, training is usually much more specific at both the prequalification and, in particular, the postqualification phases. During the latter, courses usually concentrate on specific specialisms, techniques or client groups.

This difference is probably also a reflection of employment arrangements. Within the NHS, three factors appear to have promoted generic training. Firstly, UK clinical psychologists have no system of specialist qualification so that, once employed by the NHS, they are entitled to work with any client group and to use any psychological methods and techniques. Secondly, from 1974 until 1989 in most of the UK, NHS clinical psychologists were organized into departments which provided a comprehensive service to the entire population of a locality. Thirdly, career development within the NHS normally requires a clinical psychologist to assume responsibility for planning and managing an increasingly wide range of services. There were thus obvious advantages, both to the profession and to the NHS, if all clinical psychologists obtained significant experience of each of the main client groups and specialisms.

Elsewhere in Europe, the employers of clinical psychologists, whether State agencies, local authorities, private organizations or charities, tend to provide services to specific client groups. In order to attract referrals and clients, clinical psychologists who work in independent practice will be required to demonstrate high levels of competence in specific clinical areas or techniques. In some States, advanced training in certain techniques is necessary to be able legally to practise psychotherapy, or to be eligible to have fees reimbursed by health insurance companies. In these circumstances, a 'generic' training which emphasizes breadth of experience is less adaptive than one which enables practitioners to obtain very high levels of expertise, even if only within relatively narrow clinical areas.

Entry into the profession

In most of Europe, students who have been accepted into university to study psychology will, provided they pass the examinations and any practical requirements, subsequently become qualified professional psychologists. In the UK, graduate psychologists who wish to become clinical psychologists must be selected for places on clinical training courses.

Number of entrants. The number of qualified clinical psychologists in most States is thus determined by the number of undergraduate places. In many, despite the imposition of a *numerus clausus* to restrict entry, the supply of qualified clinical psychologists has often exceeded the availability of suitable posts. One consequence is that high levels of unemployment exist, e.g. in The Netherlands, the BRD and Denmark. Another, more positive consequence is that clinical psychologists appear to have moved in larger numbers than in the UK into the less popular and the newer specialisms, e.g. learning difficulties, geropsychology, psychodiagnostics, services for drug and alcohol abusers, medical and health psychology. Many more are also in independent practice. These trends are being encouraged by some universities which, in order to increase the marketability of their students, are starting to provide more specialized training (H. F. M. Cronbag, personal communication).

In the UK, almost all the places available on postgraduate clinical training courses are funded by the NHS, with many courses making no provision for non-NHS, self-funded trainees. The crucial factor determining the size of the profession in the UK has thus been the willingness of the NHS to pay for training. For many years, the funds allocated have been insufficient to provide places for more than a small proportion (currently, one in four) of the graduate psychologists who seek clinical training. Paradoxically, many posts in the NHS are unfilled and professional developments are often inhibited because there are too few qualified clinical psychologists (MPAG, 1990).

Quality of entrants. In the UK, graduate psychologists are selected for clinical training on the basis of their personal qualities as well as their academic credentials. Elsewhere in Europe, there is usually no such filter and students can often progress to the later phase of the degree, and hence to qualification, without their personal suitability for professional practice ever having been assessed. It is to minimize any potential harmful consequences that many universities arrange courses intended to promote the personal development of students; those who specialize in clinical psychology are often expected to undergo some form of personal therapy or counselling.

Regulation of training

Prequalification phase. Certification laws are often justified as being necessary to ensure high standards of professional training. However, in those European States which have such laws, the regulatory body – usually a Government department – often appears to make little attempt to influence the content and quality of the education and training carried out prior to certification. Indeed, there may be pressure on universities to reduce the length of training and hence costs, e.g. in The Netherlands.

In the UK, the ability of the BPS to specify the form and content, and to monitor the standards, of training derives less from its own powers than from its influence on the NHS. The latter currently will employ only those clinical psychologists who have trained on 'BPS-approved' courses and, from 1993, only those who are eligible to register with the BPS as chartered clinical psychologists. The close link between the professional body and the monopolist employer thus (more than) compensates for the absence of statutory, legal regulation.

Postqualification phase. Certification laws in Europe have the major limitation that they do not influence the very significant amount of training done at the postqualification phase, much of it by private organizations. Consequently, in order to monitor and, when appropriate, to raise the standard of postqualification training, the national associations of professional psychology in several European States are becoming very active in accrediting private courses; organizing their own training courses, often in cooperation with universities; and in establishing their own postqualification credentials. By contrast, in the UK, the BPS has hardly concerned itself with postqualification clinical training. This is possibly for three reasons: the greater attention paid to the postgraduate phase; the relative absence in the UK of clinically relevant courses run by profit-making private organizations; and the role of the NHS, both in providing training for its own staff and in monitoring and enforcing professional standards.

Content of training

The greater variability in the training of clinical psychologists elsewhere in Europe, as compared with the UK, makes hazardous any generalizations about the specific content of training. One which could probably be sustained is that the role model for UK trainees is a senior clinical psychologist in the NHS, with responsibility for planning and managing a comprehensive range of services provided by more junior psychologists and for promoting the use of psychological findings and skills by other NHS staff. Thus, a list of the eight specific skills 'which fully trained UK clinical psychologists should possess' (Parry & Hall, 1988) includes: 'teaching other professions', 'consultancy skills', 'planning services' and 'evaluating services'.

In Continental Europe, these topics seldom appear in prequalification or postqualification courses. There, the role model appears to be a clinician, with advanced, specialist therapeutic or psychodiagnostic skills.

This different emphasis reflects employment conditions. The UK topics are relevant to employees working to further the aims of a service such as the NHS. They are much less central to the tasks of clinical psychologists employed by specialist units, catering only for specific client groups, or who are in independent practice and whose livelihood depends upon being perceived as having high levels of specialized and distinctive expertise.

Conclusions and prospects

Similarities and differences in training

This review has illustrated two different models of clinical psychology training, both of which begin with an education in the scientific discipline of psychology. In most of Europe, this phase is followed by an education in professional psychology and then, at the postqualification phase, usually by intensive and specialized training, often in a relatively narrow field of clinical psychology practice. By contrast, in the UK, the first phase is followed by a broad education and training in 'generic' clinical psychology, which is seldom followed by systematic postqualification training. The greater specialization which characterizes the Continental model is paralleled by its greater variability; in the UK, clinical psychologists all receive a very similar training. Other differences were noted between the UK and elsewhere, e.g. in the content of training and in the numbers trained.

Influences on training

This article considered the influence on training of three factors – the structure of higher education, the employment arrangements and the legal status of psychologists. Of these, by far the most important seems to be the employment arrangements. Many features of UK training – its focus on the prequalification phase, its commonality, its emphasis on 'breadth' rather than 'depth', some of its specific content – are all highly relevant to the goal of producing clinical psychologists to work in a salaried, managed, highly structured organization such as the NHS, responsible for providing comprehensive health care. One maladaptive feature of the UK system has been its failure to produce sufficient clinical psychologists to meet the needs even of the NHS. The system of training found elsewhere in Europe, by contrast, is well suited to the more pluralistic employment arrangements which exist there.

Interestingly, the structure of higher education reinforces these differences, e.g. in Continental Europe by requiring most of the practical training to be obtained postqualification, where greater variation is possible.

Other important influences were not discussed, such as those exercised by other professions and by the philosophical traditions which make psychologists receptive to different theoretical orientations.

Future trends

The influences outlined above are sufficiently powerful to ensure that significant differences in the practice and training of clinical psychologists will continue to exist among the various European States into the foreseeable future. However, there are other current or possible influences which might reduce these differences over the next decade. These influences are of two sorts: those which encourage the convergence of the UK and the European models and those which will affect clinical psychology practice and hence training in similar ways in many European States.

Within the UK, the changes foreshadowed by the various health White Papers (e.g. Department of Health, 1989) are resulting in more clinical psychologists working outside the NHS. Within the NHS, departments which previously provided a comprehensive service to a community are being broken up, with clinical psychologists now tending to be employed in specialist units and services. The NHS might thus see itself as having less need for generically trained clinical psychologists (although the profession might dispute this perception) and might in time come to have less influence than hitherto on the content of training. As the employment arrangements thus become more similar to those elsewhere in Europe, so might UK training change, to permit greater variability and specialization.

Conversely, the national associations of several European States, such as NIP in The Netherlands and BDP in the BRD, have been attempting to make training less individualized and more prescribed and uniform, at least at the postqualification level; in particular, practice with different client groups is being encouraged, as in the UK.

The European Community (EC) Directive 89/48/EEC 'on the mutual recognition of higher education qualifications' was recently implemented (McPherson, 1988, 1989). The example of professions, such as medicine, which were subject to earlier directives suggests that it will have a major (although possibly slow) effect on clinical psychology training, by encouraging greater harmonization of length and content. This process might eventually be reinforced, as in some other professions such as engineering, by the development of a European professional register (McPherson, 1990). Developments in higher education, such as the ERASMUS programme which promotes courses arranged jointly by universities in several States, are also likely to lead to greater harmonization of clinical training.

An example of the more general influences which might lead to similar changes throughout Europe is provided by the inter-Governmental agencies, which are becoming increasingly effective in persuading individual States to adopt common policies in sectors such as health. Thus, the World Health Organization (WHO), in its European regional strategy for Health For All (HFA), emphasizes the promotion of health and the prevention of disease by means of changing life-styles and the development of primary health care (Henderson, 1987). This strategy has been fully adopted by several European States and is influencing the health policies of most others. Of the 38 targets of HFA, psychology has been identified as being of special relevance to 20 (McPherson, 1984). WHO (e.g. Diekstra, 1989) has been emphasizing the need to reorientate clinical psychology training across Europe, so that practitioners will be better able than at present to contribute to the public health programmes proposed in HFA.

A second example of a general influence is that clinical psychologists, like all health-care professionals, are increasingly likely to come under the control of general managers, who tend to be less concerned with delineating professional roles than with defining tasks and recruiting people to undertake them, regardless of their profession (Prieto, 1992). From the WHO, Sartorius (1987) has advocated this approach as a means of improving the effectiveness of health-care systems. Clearly, its widespread adoption would have major consequences for clinical psychology training, not only in Europe but also worldwide.

While some national differences will undoubtedly remain, the changes noted above, as well as others – social, political, demographic and professional – which have not been discussed, all seem likely to lead to an increasing similarity in the content and form of clinical psychology training throughout Europe. Perhaps, in retrospect, the differences will be seen to have been at their greatest in 1992.

References

Blume, S. (1988). *The Role and Function of Universities: Postgraduate Education in the 1980's.* Paris: OECD.

Department of Health (1989). *Working for Patients,* Cm 555. London: HMSO.

Diekstra, R. F. W. (1989). Public health psychology. Paper presented to the 1st European Congress of Psychology, Amsterdam.

EFPPA (1990). *Optimal Standards for the Training of European Professional Psychologists.* Oslo: EFPPA Secretariat.

Henderson, J. H. (1987). Health for All in Europe. In H. Dent (Ed.), *Clinical Psychology: Research and Developments.* Beckenham, Kent: Croom Helm.

McPherson, F. M. (1983a). Organisation of psychological services. In A. Liddell (Ed.), *The Practice of Clinical Psychology in Great Britain.* Chichester: John Wiley.

McPherson, F. M. (1983b). The United Kingdom. *International Journal of Psychology,* **6**, 27–34.

McPherson, F. M. (1984). *Contribution of Psychology to Programme Development in WHO Regional Office for Europe.* Copenhagen: WHO Regional Office for Europe.

McPherson, F. M. (1986). The professional psychologist in Europe. *American Psychologist,* **41**, 302–305.

McPherson, F. M. (1988). Psychologists and the European Economic Community. *The Psychologist,* **1**, 353–355.

McPherson, F. M. (1989). Psychologists and the EEC (II). *The Psychologist,* **2**, 382–383.

McPherson, F. M. (1990). The regulation of a European profession of clinical psychology – some issues. *Clinical Psychology Forum,* November, 17–19.

Matarazzo, J. D. (1987). There is only one psychology, no specialities but many applications. *American Psychologist,* **42**, 893–903.

MPAG (1990). *Clinical Psychology Project: Full Report.* London: Department of Health.

Parry, G. & Hall, J. (1988). Training clinical psychologists. Paper prepared for MAS Review.

Prieto, J. M. (1992). The professionalisation process of applied psychology (in preparation).

Sartorius, N. (1987). Mental health policies and programmes for the twenty-first century. *Integrative Psychiatry,* **5**, 151–158.

British Journal of Clinical Psychology (1992), **31**, 429–443   *Printed in Great Britain*

Expressed Emotion research in Europe

Liz Kuipers*

Department of Psychology, Institute of Psychiatry, De Crespigny Park, London SE5 8AF, UK

The results of increased research into Expressed Emotion (EE) in Europe over the past five years reinforce the significance of the measure, show that it is not culturally specific and can be used with different carers including staff, and across different languages. This continuing and productive research is reviewed and new questions and issues are identified. In addition, outcome studies in schizophrenia, research in other conditions, intervention studies, methodological issues and theoretical aspects are focused on.

Expressed Emotion (EE) is a way of measuring aspects of ordinary family atmospheres (Brown, 1985), which has been found to be predictive of outcome in schizophrenia and in other conditions. As a result, social factors have been shown to be influential in a variety of psychiatric and physical conditions. It has also been possible both to mount and to evaluate intervention programmes for families with schizophrenia, the majority of which have been able to improve outcome. Until the late 1980s, research in EE had been concentrated in Britain and America. However, in the last five years, not only has interest in EE resulted in a plethora of papers, but Europe has been one of the main contributors. In this review, I will concentrate on papers written since 1987, and only research based in a European country will be discussed. This is not to deny the importance of work done elsewhere, such as in Australia, North and South America, Japan and India, but merely to provide a focus in the year of Europe 1992.

EE is rated from an audiotape of an interview with a carer. This interview, abbreviated by Vaughn & Leff (1976) and called the Camberwell Family Interview (CFI), has a semi-structured format, which allows a flexible use of standard questions and probes and encourages an interviewer to listen to information as it emerges, and not to interrupt if areas of interest have been spontaneously discussed. The interview covers the start of problems, focuses on the previous three months, and asks about other areas of relationships, such as irritability and tension. Symptoms and coping responses are discussed; recent examples are probed for if a carer is reticent or vague. How time is spent in a typical week is the basis of what is called the time budget, which allows assessment of time awake spent in the same room together for the patient and carer. The content, but more importantly the vocal aspects of speech, are rated from the interview. This novel way of rating speech appears to be one of the reasons for EE's predictiveness; the use of vocal attributes such as speed, pitch and

* Requests for reprints.

emphasis in delivery appears to allow emotional aspects to be picked up regardless of specific content.

From the CFI five scales can be rated. These are critical comments (CC), positive remarks (PR), (both frequency ratings), and global ratings of hostility (H), warmth (W), and emotional overinvolvement (EOI). Of these CC, H, and EOI have been the most predictive of relapse and many studies now do not discuss W and PR. CC rely particularly on tone, and are defined as an unfavourable remark about a person's behaviour or personality. CC are usually the most prevalent rating. H can exist independently of CC, but is often associated with criticism – it is defined either as a generalization of criticism (rating of 1), or as a rejecting remark (rating of 2), and relies on content which is usually unequivocal. If both generalization and rejection are present, a rating of 3 is given. EOI is the most complex of the scales, combining aspects of overprotection, self-sacrifice and past exaggerated emotional response as well as behaviour during the interview (such as crying) and dramatization (such as extravagant praise, the tone and tempo of speech). Traditionally, the scales have been used as categories; high EE is defined either as criticism exceeding a cut-off of $\geqslant 6$ CC, or as a moderate amount of EOI ($\geqslant \frac{3}{5}$) or as any hostility (maximum 3). Some carers will exhibit a mixture of these high ratings. They define a family as high EE even if only one member is so rated. The cut-off points are not standard. They have mainly arisen either as medians, or as the most predictive level for that sample. This has meant that cut-offs vary. This continues to cause problems of comparability across studies, although as Kavanagh (1992) points out: 'the data do not support the contention that EE results are significantly affected by changing criteria' (p. 603). The use of categories has itself been criticized as inappropriate for this kind of data, but is now so 'institutionalized' that studies continue the practice. Both the genesis of the measure and its development have been extensively reviewed elsewhere and will not be considered here (see Kavanagh, 1992; Kuipers & Bebbington, 1988; Lam, 1991; Leff & Vaughn, 1985).

Looking at European studies, six categories suggest themselves. Firstly and most prolifically, there have been replications of the effect of EE on outcome in schizophrenia. Secondly, conditions other than schizophrenia have been studied. Thirdly, there are intervention studies. Fourthly, the attitudes of other carers, such as staff, have been considered. Fifthly, there has been interest in methodological issues; validity, stability of the measures and other ways of measuring EE apart from the Camberwell Family Interview (CFI). Finally, in Europe there is an undercurrent of concern about EE being 'atheoretical', a concern picked up from an anthropological viewpoint by Jenkins (1991). Evidence for this will also be considered.

1. Outcome in schizophrenia

This is the most notable feature of European EE research, both in terms of the number of studies and, more interestingly, in terms of the high degree of replication that they demonstrate across a variety of languages and cultures. Kavanagh (1992) has also looked at this area and, as he points out, most of the recent replications have been in the predicted direction, i.e. high EE in a relative is associated with higher risk of relapse in schizophrenia in the 9–12 months after discharge from hospital: 'the median relapse rate is 21 per cent for low EE or less than half of the 48 per cent rate in the high EE group' (p. 601). This recent confirmatory research is almost all

European. As well as those studies mentioned by Kavanagh, some others, not all published, demonstrate similar effects. The last five years of European studies on outcome encompass eight different languages and are shown in Table 1.

Table 1. European research on outcome studies in schizophrenia since 1987

Authors	N	Country	9 month % relapse rate (Total N)	
			High EE	Low EE
Gutierrez et al. (1988)[a]	32	Spain	54 (11)	10 (21)
Arevalo & Vizcarro (1989)[a]	31	Spain	44 (18)	38 (13)
Ivanovic & Valetic (1989)	60	Belgrade, Yugoslavia	65 (29)	7 (31)
Rostworowska et al. (1989) Budzyna-Dawidowski et al. (1989)	36	Poland	60 (25)	30 (11)
Barrelet et al. (1990)	36	Switzerland (French)	33 (24)	0 (12)
Buchremer et al. (1991)[a]	99	Germany	37 (59)	28 (40)
Stirling et al. (1991)[b]	33	Manchester, England 1st admission or early onset patients only	31 (16)	47 (17)
Bertrando et al. (1992)[c]	42	Milan, Italy	14 (24)	4 (18)
Cohen, Niedermeier & Watzl (1992)	64	Germany	significant difference only at 12 months after discharge	
Montero et al. (1992)	60	Spain	40 (30)	12 (30)
Mozny & Votypkova (1992)	125	Czechoslovakia	59 (69)	23 (56)

[a] Figures from Kavanagh (1992) p. 602.
[b] Relapse 12 months after discharge.
[c] Relapse = hospital admission and cut-off for EOI ⩾ 7.4.

Stirling, Tantam, Thomas, Newby & Montague's study (1991), in Britain, was one of the few that failed to find evidence for an association between high EE and relapse, although correlates between components of EE and premorbid measures were significant, in a population characterized by first admission or early onset patients and predominantly high EOI relatives. Barrelet, Favre, Ferrero, Haynal, Hooton & Szigethy (1992) make the point that a narrow definition of relapse is necessary for a clear relationship between EE and poor outcome to emerge.

Mavreas, Tomaras, Karydi, Economon & Stefanis (1992) have so far only completed baseline rather than outcome measures on 75 patients and 121 relatives in Athens, Greece. Fifty-eight per cent of all relatives were low EE and 26 per cent were only EOI using a rating of ⩾ 4 on EOI, 12 per cent were critical, 2.5 per cent were critical and EOI and 1.5 per cent were hostile. In the early studies, high EOI alone accounted for only 5 per cent of relatives (Kuipers, 1979). The reversal of the proportion of EOI and criticism in this population and in the Stirling study suggests that in some populations EOI is a noticeable feature. Jenkins (1991) argues that EOI in particular is able to transcend cultural boundaries because it can be adapted to new cultural norms; in other words, for high levels of EOI to be rated in a different culture a relative's behaviour should be culturally unusual, or violate cultural rules. This is not simply a matter of changing cut-off points, but reflects a fundamental aspect of the rating – EOI is meant to be rating *over*concern, not ordinary or normal responses, so that in a different culture unusual responses can potentially be identified by an indigenous rater. However, this aspect has not been formalized for different cultures and it is not clear in the Mavreas study what definitions were given to the extreme end of the EOI scale, the benchmarks, that were used to rate EOI in Greece. Nor do we yet know if EOI is predictive of outcome in schizophrenia in this population. If it is, then it suggests that intervention geared to dealing with this aspect would be particularly necessary in this population.

Jenkins (1991) is also illuminating in discussing criticism. She points out that critical comments (CC) focus on vocal characteristics and rely on content only if it is unequivocal: '...vocal markers, although their use varies from culture to culture (Irvine, 1990) are observed to function in many languages...distinguishing, for example, between teasing and criticism (Ochs, 1986)' (p. 398). It seems likely that this emphasis on such common features of speech has enabled criticism to be picked up in very different European languages. It also seems possible that the lack of specificity of the content of CC allows different cultures to criticize a variety of attributes in their ill relatives. Although few studies have yet carried out a content analysis of their ratings, it could be hypothesized that this might vary across countries, and yet not affect the predictiveness of the measure.

Other studies, either showing preliminary results or only just beginning, suggest similar findings to those already completed. Llovet (1991), in Spain, found a relationship between EE and relapse in patients with schizophrenia. Pumar *et al.* (1991), looking at 50 Spanish families with a member with schizophrenia, found that high EOI mothers were perceived as overprotective by patients, but had low care behaviours. Orhagen & d'Elia (1991) used the CFI on 32 relatives in Sweden, and rated around two-thirds as high in EE. Finally, Bentsen (1992) and colleagues in Oslo, Norway, have just started a study looking at EE, relatives' attributions about patient illness, patient and relative perceptions and outcome in schizophrenia.

These outcome studies raise several issues. It is not clear from the data available to what extent EOI varies across cultures. If it does vary, is this due to natural and potentially interesting aspects of different cultures, or to variation in the so far subjective rater decisions about 'unusual' responses to mental illness in different cultures? Investigation of this would require that ratings were formalized and examples of extreme ratings discussed and agreed on, when a new language is being investigated. This remains to be done. The second issue is whether EOI is itself predictive of relapse. If it is the major determinant of high EE, instead of criticism, how does this alter our understanding of the association between high EE and relapse in different cultures? There is also an issue concerning cut-off points, particularly for EOI. At this stage, a standard cut-off, say 3 or more, used in the majority of studies, should really be more consistently applied, so that results in different countries can be compared.

In conclusion, however, the last five years of outcome studies in Europe tend to confirm what has been found elsewhere, that the EE measure remains a robust predictor of relapse in schizophrenia and is able to identify 'stressful' environments across cultures.

2. Other conditions

Schizophrenia is not the only condition whose relationship to EE has been examined. European research has also focused on manic depression, eating disorders and a variety of non-psychiatric conditions. Bressi & Invernizzi (1991), from Italy, presented preliminary results of a study where they administered the CFI to relatives of patients with both acute and chronic physical illness. They found that levels of EE were higher in relatives of kidney transplant and breast cancer patients than in relatives of those with schizophrenia but lower in relatives of heart disease patients. They also report that high EOI, when correlated with high warmth, was positively perceived by patients, but high EOI, when combined with criticism and hostility, had a poor influence on the patients' acceptance of their illness.

Flanagan & Wagner (1991) in Manchester, England, looked at EE in 30 key relatives of severely obese patients when they were at the beginning of a restricted diet programme. After five months on the diet, patients living with a high EE relative were much less likely to comply with treatment. Obese patients also showed higher levels of anxiety than matched controls, although a combination of high anxiety and a high EE relative did not improve the prediction of treatment compliance over having a high EE relative alone. Interestingly, as in Mavreas *et al's* study (1992), which rated over a quarter of relatives as high on EOI, 6/14 (42 per cent) of husbands were high on EOI (three were critical, and five were low EE); 2/9 parents were high on EOI (five were critical, two low EE); and three wives were all low EE (no information was given on the remaining relatives).

Van Furth (1991) in Utrecht, Holland, looked at a population of 63 anorexic and bulimic patients. EE levels in 84 parents of 46 families with an eating disorder were rated on EE using both the CFI and five-minute speech sample (FMSS) (Magana *et al.*, 1986). Szmukler, Eisler, Russell & Dare (1985) had previously found that high EE was predictive of drop-out in therapy for anorexia. Van Furth found that greater maternal critical attitudes were related to poorer outcome after therapy, and that high levels of paternal warmth were related to the patients' body mass at follow-up. One of the other variables Van Furth looked at was the personality attributes of parents using the Dutch Personality Questionnaire (DPQ), which measures seven characteristics: neuroticism, social anxiety, rigidity, hostility, egotism, dominance and self-esteem. He found that anorexic parental DPQ scores were comparable to the norm, and concluded that high EE was not related to 'character pathology' (p. 129) in anorexic patients' parents. Espina, Pumar, Bel, Santos & Elortegui (1991), in Spain, reported a similar lack of relationship between EE, depression, anxiety or personality variables (EPQ) in families with schizophrenia. Both findings corroborate George Brown's intention (1985) that EE should be picking up 'ordinary' rather than 'pathological' family interactions.

Hooley & Teasdale (1989), in a sample of unipolar depressives, found both EE in spouses and marital distress were significantly associated with nine-month relapse rates in patients, using a cut-off point of two critical comments. They also pointed out that the single best predictor of relapse in this sample was patients' perception of criticism in the spouse.

Priebe, Wildgrube & Muller-Oerlinghausen (1989, 1992*a*) investigated 21 key relatives of 15 patients with bipolar affective or schizoaffective psychoses. Patients had been on continuous prophylactic lithium treatment for at least three years and were asymptomatic at the nine-month interview. Relatives were interviewed with the CFI initially and then again after more than two years (28 months). Two critical comments were used as the cut-off for a high EE relative. Because of death and drop-out, only 15 relatives were interviewed at follow-up. In the first study (1989), Priebe and colleagues found high EE in relatives predicted significantly poorer response during the three years before interview and the subsequent nine months. In the follow-up study, morbidity indices in the remaining high EE relatives (10/15) were four to 10 times higher than in the low EE group. Two relatives had spontaneously changed from high to low EE during the follow-up, a number consistent with that found previously (Leff, Kuipers, Berkowitz, Eberlein-Fries & Sturgeon, 1982). The authors concluded that patients living with consistently low EE relatives rarely need intervention in addition to medication. Although this is a small sample, it confirms ideas that high EE families are a high-risk group in particular need of social intervention.

Priebe and colleagues (1992*b*) have also looked at EE in partners of 32 patients with coronary heart disease. Again, two critical comments were used to define high EE relatives. EE did not predict outcome after nine months of rehabilitation. However, high and low EE relatives (relatives were only critical; the one relative high in EOI was classified as low EE in this study) did differ in their attitudes to the illness, in that high EE partners considered psychological factors as more important for the illness than did low EE partners. Patients with high EE partners had a higher familial risk of heart disease, and they were also more depressed at the beginning of the rehabilitation. The authors were not able to offer an explanation for either of these findings from their data.

Marks, Wieck, Seymour, Checkley & Kumar, (in press), in Britain, carried out EE interviews with the partners of 25 women with a previous episode of psychosis or severe depression. Interviews were done when the women were 36 weeks pregnant. Unusually they found that the number of positive remarks was the best predictor of subsequent postnatal affective relapse. In fact, those who had partners who were least critical and also made the least positive comments (less than two positive remarks; less than three critical comments were the cut-off points) relapsed most, compared to a control and to the 'well' group. The authors called a subgroup of these 'uncommunicative' partners (no positive or critical comments). Their results suggest a different mechanism may be operating for these husbands and also corroborate Peter & Hand's (1988) study, where patients with high EE spouses showed *fewer* agoraphobic symptoms at follow-up than those with low EE partners.

Sensky, Stevenson, Magrill & Petty (1991) looked at EE in 40 families who included an adolescent with diabetes. They note that it was possible to adapt the CFI for this population, and found a range of EE attitudes in the 80 parents. Mothers and fathers tended to have similar ratings, and parents who attributed problem behaviour to diabetes were significantly less critical than other parents. As yet, there are no published data on outcome from this study.

Bledin, MacCarthy, Kuipers, & Woods (1990) investigated EE levels in daughters who were caring for a parent with dementia. The median of four critical comments was used as a cut-off point to define high EE in carers. Very little overinvolvement was rated. Carers rated high on EE, who were critical and also often hostile, were significantly more likely to report higher levels of strain and distress. More effective coping strategies were shown by carers who made fewer critical comments and more positive remarks. Again, however, there was no definite link between high EE and poor outcome, despite a death rate of 20 per cent in the parents over the subsequent nine months. Finally, Vaughn (1992) is measuring EE in carers of those with inflammatory bowel disease, although no significant links have been found between EE in key relatives and the course of the illness.

These studies continue to show that the CFI can be successfully adapted to a wide range of other conditions, using relatively few changes in the content or wording of the interview. It is not yet clear, however, whether EOI has been rated consistently in different illnesses. EOI relies on a rating of overprotective and overconcerned behaviour, which may be specific to that condition, and relies on a rater's knowledge of ordinary rather than unusual coping responses in carers. Nevertheless, EE ratings, whether due to criticism or emotional overinvolvement, are often linked with a poor outcome, although some studies (e.g. Marks *et al.*, 1992) redefine high EE in unusual ways. Even if no links with outcome are found, high EE in carers tends to be associated with more distress and worry and this may suggest useful ways of intervening in the future with these groups.

3. Intervention studies

These have been extensively reviewed elsewhere (Kavanagh, 1992; Kuipers & Bebbington, 1988; Lam, 1991). Interventions since 1987 have been either British (Tarrier *et al.*, 1988*b*, 1989; Leff *et al.*, 1989, 1990), American (Hogarty *et al.*, 1986; Hogarty, Anderson & Reiss, 1987), or Australian (Vaughan *et al.*, 1992). The only exception to this is a study in Sweden which offered education, family groups and family meetings to 23 relatives and reduced their EE levels, although, unfortunately, no information on patients was included (Orhagen, d'Elia & Gustafsson, 1992). Recent British intervention studies have shown that education by itself did not affect outcome, and that there was no advantage in different kinds of behavioural intervention, both enactive and symbolic treatment groups being equally effective in reducing relapse rates in patients (Tarrier *et al.*, 1988*b*). The Leff study (1989) looked at differences between education and individual family work and education and a relative's group. They also found no significant difference between these two treatments in patients' relapse rates over nine months, although small numbers may make it hard to interpret this finding. However, there was a difference in take-up, in that it was more difficult to engage carers in the relatives' group. This suggests that while relatives' groups can be cost effective (two therapists can see several families in one place) there will always be some families who require the home visiting of individual family treatment.

An earlier British study on long-term patients and relatives which had shown an impact, offered carers education and a monthly relatives group, and was able to reduce EE, improve coping, reported social behaviour in patients, and feelings of reciprocity (MacCarthy *et al.*, 1989*a*; Kuipers, MacCarthy, Hurry & Harper, 1989).

However, a Scottish study by MacCreadie *et al.* (1991) attempted intervention on the lines suggested by previous studies, but without specific training, and was not particularly effective, although patient relapses did decrease after intervention and relatives who received it were positive about it. Vaughan *et al's* (1992) study, although conducted in Australia, is useful in helping to elucidate why an intervention may not be effective. They offered parents of 36 patients 10 weeks of counselling, which did not include the patient. This did not significantly reduce relapse rates compared to a control group who received standard aftercare. The authors suggest that in order to improve outcome for patients and their families interventions need to be focused, include the patient and an individual needs assessment, liaise with the clinical team, continue for some time and use adequately trained staff. While all these features may not be necessary, it looks likely that a successful intervention must include a sufficient number of them. While it is still not clear what the minimum requirements of effective interventions are, it probably is clear that studies that make assumptions such as that staff can deliver social interventions without specific training, or that any social intervention is better than none, will fail. Questions of cost effective and optimal interventions remain to be answered, in Europe as elsewhere.

4. EE in staff

An interesting extension of the EE research, both in Britain and the rest of Europe, has been to consider EE in other carers, notably staff. Typically, the staff involved have shared some of the characteristics of other carers, because they have been the key workers with patients in long-term care, and thus not only have spent time with patients but have also had a working relationship with the client of at least three months. In research into burden, it has been found that staff and relatives share the impact of many of the behaviour problems and disturbance of clients but, unlike relatives, staff have time off and holidays, i.e. respite, which relatives often ask for but rarely receive (MacCarthy *et al.*, 1989 *b*).

A series of studies, still ongoing in Britain, have shown that staff emit a range of EE attitudes, and that over 40 per cent ($N = 35$) of staff had a high rating (more than six critical comments was the high EE cut-off) about at least one key patient (Moore, Ball & Kuipers, 1992*a*). This replicates an unpublished finding by Watts (1988) in England and has also been found in a study in Germany by Herzog (1992) who reported the majority of staff to be high EE. In Italy, Beltz *et al.* (1991) showed that there was no consistent relationship between staff and family levels of EE. In other words, individual patients were not reliably associated with a high EE response in all their carers, although both staff and family members did show high EE attitudes. In a content analysis of the 61 interviews elicited from 35 staff members (Moore, Kuipers & Ball, 1992*b*), criticism was most frequently focused in both high and low EE interviews on socially embarrassing or difficult behaviour, and on the clinical poverty syndrome, e.g. apathy, slowness, and poor self-care (Wykes, 1982). The category which attracted the most criticism was the repetition of inappropriate behaviour and attention seeking. This mirrors a result found in the dementia study, that the behaviour most often criticized by carers was repetitious speech and behaviour (Bledin *et al.*, 1990). In staff, high levels of criticism were significantly related to regarding the patients' difficulties as under their own control, and having negative rather than positive expectations of a patient's ability to manage independently. A further prospective naturalistic study of differential outcome in two hostels, one characterized by a majority of high EE staff, the other by low EE staff, suggested that patients in the former hostel had a poorer outcome in the subsequent nine months (Ball, Moore, & Kuipers, 1992).

A final, unpublished, study used the five-minute speech sample (FMSS) to look at staff attitudes towards patients after a violent incident. The FMSS rates EE from an uninterrupted five minutes of speech, using slightly expanded criteria of negative affect and EE (Magana *et al.*, 1986). Twenty staff involved in a violent incident showed raised levels of EE towards the violent patient and raised anxiety in the subsequent month (Cottle, Kuipers & Murphy, 1992). The studies on staff emphasize that it is not just relatives who can have high levels of EE towards patients, and that anyone in a relationship, even a professional one, with someone with long-term difficulties such as schizophrenia, may not find it easy to be tolerant and to cope well. The research indicates again, not only that the CFI can be adapted in a variety of ways but also that EE ratings can identify other carers who find the caring role frustrating. It also seems to be true that some patients are particularly difficult to like, i.e. those who show less warmth and reciprocation (Moore *et al.*, 1992*a*). These patients may need to be given individual consideration in order to ensure that they too receive high quality care. It may be that in order to work effectively with a very disabled client group, staff should concentrate on clients' positive and likeable features as a deliberate way of fostering the ability to provide adequate and effective care for them.

5. Methodological issues

A small number of European studies have been concerned with these issues. Fevre, Gonzales & Lendais (1989) looked at the stability of EE over a nine-month period in 35 relatives of 22 patients with schizophrenia. They found reasonably good evidence for the stability of the measure, with the majority of relatives being either stable high or low EE. However, there was also a proportion of unstable relatives who typically displayed fewer critical comments (6–10) than the stable high EE groups. The authors point out that few of the changes that were observed in EE levels depended on the clinical state of patients. This finding confirms the idea that there are three groups of relatives: those who are low EE and cope well, those who are low EE and become high EE under stress, and those who are continuously high EE (Kuipers & Bebbington, 1990). However, more evidence is needed for this proposition. The temporal stability of the EE measure needs to be investigated properly, together with the covariation of relatives' levels of burden and coping skills, and patients' levels of symptomatology and social functioning. There is already some preliminary evidence that high EE and burden are related over nine months (Smith, Birchwood, Cochrane & George, 1992), and that high EE is related to low social functioning in patients (Barrowclough & Tarrier, 1990).

In terms of measurement itself, there is continuing interest in the FMSS as an alternative to the CFI for measuring EE levels. Its obvious brevity makes it attractive, but raters have to have some idea of what criticism is, which means that training is still required. Its main shortcoming, also reported by Van Furth (1991), is that it 'misses' up to 25 per cent of those rated as high EE on the CFI; i.e. it is too brief and can only clearly rate as high EE those who are unequivocally so. Whether a version with more prompts would have better sensitivity and specificity is currently being investigated (Bentson, 1992).

The issue of what EE is and what it relates to has also been looked at. Hubschmid & Zemp (1989), in Austria, rated 17 parents of schizophrenic patients on EE using the CFI, and also used a semi-structured interview to ask them about interactions with the patient. Transcripts of the latter were analysed using the structural analysis of social behaviour (SASB). They found that a high EE relationship had a more negative emotional climate, a conflict-prone structure and rigid patterns of interaction. On the other hand, 'low EE relationships were not only less critical but also make significantly more emotionally positive and supportive statements' (p. 116). This study confirms the view that low EE relationships are not neutral, but have positive and beneficial effects on patients.

Hegerl, Priebe, Wildgrube & Muller-Oerlinghausen (1990) looked at auditory evoked potentials in high and low EE non-biological relatives of affective psychosis patients. Low EE relatives demonstrated steeper slopes in the amplitude/intensity functions. This study together with the eloctrodermal results of Tarrier *et al.* (1988 *a*) and Tarrier (1989), who found decreases in electrodermal activity when patients were in the presence of a low EE relative, suggest further that low EE relatives may have particular ways of reducing 'arousal' or stress associated with interactions.

Brewin, MacCarthy, Duda & Vaughn (1991), in Britain, related EE in 58 relatives to their spontaneous expressions of causal beliefs about the illness of the patients (who had schizophrenia) and their negative behaviour. They found that low EE relatives made attributions similar to EOI relatives. However, critical relatives made more attributions to factors that were personal to and controllable by the patient. Hostile relatives were further characterized by attributions internal to the patient (such as laziness) and by making attributions with fewer causal elements (e.g. negative events caused solely by the patient). These results confirm that poorly informed and poorly supported relatives are likely to make a wide variety of attributional responses to an illness such as schizophrenia which does not have certain causes. It further suggests that these are key factors in the change that takes place during structured interventions, and in particular that the education component of intervention is a fundamental part of this.

Finally, there is a study on the Level of Expressed Emotion Scale (LEE) by Gerlsma, Van de Lubbe, & Van Nieuwen-Huizen (1992). This scale is meant to measure patients' perceptions of EE, although in this study EE itself was not rated. The authors identify lack of emotional support, intrusiveness, control and instability as the components which best describe their data following factor analysis. However, as the authors point out, neither the relation of the scale to the EE measure nor its predictive power have yet been investigated.

6. Theoretical aspects

With the exception of Britain, European research on EE has tended to lag behind American research, and it is possible to detect a cautious rather than an enthusiastic acceptance of the concept. This has changed in recent years, with most research on EE now centred in Europe. However, a concern remains that EE is only a measure and that even the resulting interventions, although successful in the main, have been pragmatic not 'theoretical'.

Angermeyer (1987) suggested three theoretical concepts associated with EE: a measure of chronic stress (Brown, Birley & Wing, 1972), of social control (Greenley, 1986), or the quality of social support (Beels, Gutwirth, Berkeley & Struening, 1984). In a later review, Lam (1991) stated that despite the intervention studies being 'empirically driven' there are theories that encompass them; these include coping, stress and attribution theories. Jenkins & Karno (1992) are more trenchant. They point out that an explanation of EE 'requires a theoretical bridge from behaviour to meaning' (p. 12). They go on to speculate that 'In our view, the unknown and theoretically overarching something or somethings indexed by the global construct of EE are culturally constituted features of kin response to an ill relative' (p. 16). They thus conclude that 'a theoretical accounting of what is inside the "black box" called EE must therefore prominently concern the concept of culture' (p. 16). This view seems to articulate what many European researchers also feel. However, to suggest that culture will provide all the answers to the 'black box' of EE seems to put the case too strongly. While cultural aspects have been surprisingly muted in the EE research, with emphasis on differences in EE levels rather than on meaning, and while elucidation of meaning would undoubtedly be of interest, it is not clear that this anthropological view is any more than part of our understanding.

As George Brown (1985) discusses in his retrospective view of how EE was 'discovered', the measure is not atheoretical. It seems likely that a measure is only required because there is a theory. Why else would one investigate and look at data, if not to inform an idea, based on some theory of how the data might be organized? The trouble with research into social factors, of which EE is a part, is that the theory is a low level one; i.e. the idea that social aspects might have an influence on illness as severe as schizophrenia now seems entirely reasonable, but was not in the 1950s when Brown and colleagues were pursuing it. As Brown describes, although they did not know *which* areas of family life would be important, they had clearly identified that ordinary aspects of family life, to which almost everyone would be subject, would be likely to be central. Brown uses the term 'retroduction' for the method of inspecting anomalies in the data which then enable new predictions to be made and tested.

The EE measure thus arose as a reliable and valid way of measuring family atmosphere in order to test the predictions effectively. One might find a parallel in the measurement of blood pressure, which is an indirect way of accessing the rate of the flow of blood. It too, once measured, reliably predicts poor outcome in some individuals. We now know a great deal more both about the reasons for this and about possible palliatives and treatments, whose effects can be assessed. Perhaps EE should be seen as the 'blood pressure' of family life, which allows one to tap into possible difficulties and does not preclude other measures, nor more sophisticated explanations emerging as to the reasons behind it.

Conclusions

European EE research now spans all the major issues in an expanding number of countries, although major intervention studies so far have been conducted only in Britain. The fact that this is so reflects the many hours of training in EE that have gone on, again mainly in Britain, and also the fact that as long as researchers can understand and speak English, it is possible to transfer the rating and interview techniques across many different settings, and across different carers.

The successful transfer of the measure suggests that the EE research could be a new way of looking at the impact of severe conditions in different cultures. This aspect has yet to be developed, however, because emphasis in the rest of Europe so far has been on showing that EE exists and is predictive of relapse. Further, the fact that EE does seem to transcend language barriers potentially gives a new understanding of the concept of EE both in terms of its definition and in the way that carers cope with unusual and difficult problems in those they live with. This aspect has also yet to be looked at in any detail.

The number of and interest in EE studies gives substance to the idea that the measure has enabled progressive research which is not atheoretical; it leads to new predictions, new tests of ideas and to intervention studies which have the advantage of being empirically testable. It seems likely that these latter will be the next focus of continuing research on EE in Europe.

Acknowledgements

I would like to thank Dr C. Vaughn and D. Lam for their comments.

References

Angermeyer, M. C. (1987). Theoretical implications of psychosocial intervention studies on schizophrenia. In H. Hafner, W. Gattaz & W. Janzavik (Eds), *Search for the Causes of Schizophrenia*. Berlin: Springer-Verlag.

Arevalo, J. & Vizcarro, C. (1989). Emocion Expresada y curso de la esquizofrenia en una numestra espanola. *Analisis y Modificación de Conducta*, **15**, 3–23.

Ball, R. A., Moore, E. & Kuipers, L. (1992). EE in community care facilities: a comparison of patient outcome in a 9 month follow-up of two residential hostels. *Social Psychiatry and Psychiatric Epidemiology*, **27**, 35–39.

Barrelet, L., Ferrero, F., Szigethy, L., Giddey, C. & Pellizzer, G. (1990). EE and first admission schizophrenia: Nine month follow-up in a French cultural environment. *British Journal of Psychiatry*, **156**, 357–362.

Barrelet, L., Favre, S., Ferrero, F., Haynal, A., Hooton, A. & Szigethy, L. (1992). EE and schizophrenia relapse. *British Journal of Psychiatry* (in press).

Barrowclough, C. and Tarrier, N. (1990). Social functioning in schizophrenic patients: I The effects of EE and family intervention. *Social Psychiatry and Psychiatric Epidemiology*, **25**, 125–129.

Beels, C. C., Gutwirth, L., Berkeley, J. & Struening, E. (1984). Measurements of social support in schizophrenia. *Schizophrenia Bulletin*, **10**, 399–411.

Beltz, J., Bertrando, P., Clerici, M., Albertini, E., Merati, O. & Cazullo, C. L. (1991). Emotiva Espresso e schizoprenia: Dai familiari agli operatori psychiatrici. Symposium on Expressed Emotion in Latin based languages. Barcelona, Spain.

Bentson, H. (1992). The Blakstad-Ganstad family project: Schizophrenia and Expressed Emotion in the family. Oslo, Norway. Personal communication.

Bertrando, P., Bressi, C., Cereda, G., Clerici, M., Farma, T. & Cazullo, C. L. (1992). Expressed Emotion and schizophrenia in Italy: A study of an Italian urban population. Personal communication.

Bledin, K., MacCarthy, B., Kuipers, L. & Woods, R. (1990). Daughters of people with dementia: EE, strain and coping. *British Journal of Psychiatry*, **157**, 221–227.

Bressi, C. and Invernizzi, G. (1991). L'emotivita espresca nelle famiglie di Malati organici: significato e limiti. Symposium on Expressed Emotion in Latin based languages. Barcelona, Spain.

Brewin, C. R., MacCarthy, B., Duda, K. & Vaughn, C. E. (1991). Attribution and Expressed Emotion in the relatives of patients with schizophrenia. *Journal of Abnormal Psychology*, **100**, 546–554.

Brown, G. (1985). The discovery of EE: Induction or deduction? In J. Leff & C. Vaughn, *Expressed Emotion in Families*. New York: Guilford.

Brown, G. W., Birley, J. L. & Wing, J. K. (1972). Influence of family life on the course of schizophrenic illness: A replication. *British Journal of Psychiatry*, **121**, 241–258.

Buchremer, G., Stricker, K., Holle, R. & Kuhs, H. (1991). The predictability of relapse in schizophrenia patients. *European Archives of Psychiatry and Clinical Neurosciences* **240**, 292–300.

Budzyna-Dawidowski, P., Rostworowska, M. & Barbaro, B. (1989). Stability of Expressed Emotion: A 3 year follow-up study of psychiatric patients. Paper presented to XIX Congress of Behaviour Therapy. Vienna, Austria.

Cohen, R., Niedermeier, T. & Watzl, H. (1992). Expressed Emotion and relapse rates in schizophrenic patients. Personal communication.

Cottle, M., Kuipers, L. & Murphy, G. (1992). Expressed Emotion attributions and coping in staff victims of violence. Unpublished manuscript, Institute of Psychiatry, London.

Espina, A., Pumar, B., Bel, A., Santos, A. & Elortegui, G. Y. A. (1991). Emocion expresada y caracteristicas de personalidad, psicopatologicas y de ajuste diadico en padres de hijos esquizofrenicos. Symposium on Expressed Emotion in Latin based languages. Barcelona, Spain.

Fevre, S., Gonzales, C. & Lendais, G. (1989). Expressed Emotion of schizophrenics' relatives. Poster presented at VIIIth World Congress of Psychiatry. Athens, Greece.

Flanagan, D. A. J. & Wagner, H. L. (1991). Expressed Emotion and panic–fear in the prediction of diet treatment compliance. *British Journal of Clinical Psychology*. **30**, 231–240.

Gerlsma, C., Van de Lubbe, P. M. & Van Nieuwen-Huizen, C. (1992). Factor analysis of the level of Expressed Emotion Scale: A questionnaire intended to measure 'perceived EE'. *British Journal of Psychiatry*, **160**, 385–389.

Greenley, J. R. (1986) Social control and EE. *Journal of Nervous and Mental Disorders*, **174**, 24–30.

Gutierrez, E., Escudero, V. & Valero, J. A. (1988). Expresion de emociones y curso de la esquizofrenia: II Expresion de emociones y curso de la esquizofrenia en pacientes en remision. *Analisis y modificación de Conducta*, **14**, 275–316.

Hegerl, U., Priebe, S, Wildgrube, C. & Muller-Oerlinghausen, B. (1990). Expresed Emotion and auditory evoked potentials. *Psychiatry*, **53**, 108–114.

Herzog (1992). Nurses, patients and relatives: A study of family patterns on psychiatric wards. In C. L. Cazzullo and G. Invernizzi (Eds), *Family Intervention in Schizophrenia: Experiences and Orientations in Europe*. Milan: ARS (in press).

Hogarty, G. E., Anderson, C. M., Reiss, D. J., Kornblith, S. J., Greenwald, D. P., Javna, C. D. & Madonia, M. J. (1986). Family psycho-education, social skills training and maintenance chemotherapy in the aftercare treatment of schizophrenia. I. One year effects of a controlled study on relapse and Expressed Emotion. *Archives of General Psychiatry*, **43**, 633–642.

Hogarty, G. E., Anderson, C. M. & Reiss, D. J. (1987). Family psycho-education, social skills training, and medication in schizophrenia: The long and the short of it. *Psychopharmacology Bulletin*, **23**, 12–13.

Hooley, J. & Teasdale, J. (1989). Predictors of relapse in unipolar depressives, EE, marital distress and perceived criticism. *Journal of Abnormal Psychology*, **98**, 229–235.

Hubschmid, T. & Zemp, M. (1989). Interaction in high and low Expressed Emotion families. *Social Psychiatry and Psychiatric Epidemiology*, **24**, 113–119.

Irvine, J. (1990). Registering affect: Heteroglossia in the linguistic expression of emotion. In C. Lutz and L. Abu-Lughod (Eds), *Language and Politics of Emotion*, pp. 126–161. Cambridge: Cambridge University Press.

Ivanovic, M. & Valetic, Z. (1989). Expressed Emotion in families of patients with frequent types of schizophrenia and influence on the course of illness: Nine months follow-up. Paper presented at XIX Congress of European Association of Behaviour Therapy. Vienna, Austria.

Jenkins, J. H. (1991). Anthropology: Expressed Emotion and schizophrenia. *Ethos*, **19**, 387–431.

Jenkins, J. H. & Karno, M. (1992). The meaning of Expressed Emotion: Theoretical issues raised by cross cultural research. *American Journal of Psychology*, **149**, 9–21.

Kavanagh, D. J. (1992). Recent developments in Expressed Emotion and schizophrenia. *British Journal of Psychiatry*, **160**, 601–620.

Kuipers, L. (1979). Expressed Emotion: A review. *British Journal of Social and Clinical Psychology*, **18**, 237–243.

Kuipers, L. & Bebbington, P. E. (1988). Expressed Emotion research in schizophrenia: theoretical and clinical implications. *Psychological Medicine*, **18**, 893–910.

Kuipers, L. & Bebbington, P. E. (1990). *Working in Partnership: Clinicians and Carers in the Management of Long-standing Mental Illness*. Oxford: Heinemann Medical.

Kuipers, L., MacCarthy, B., Hurry, J. & Harper, R. (1989). A low cost supportive model for relatives of the long term adult mentally ill. *British Journal of Psychiatry*, **154**, 775–782.

Lam, D. H. (1991). Psychological family intervention in schizophrenia: A review of empirical studies. *Psychological Medicine*, **21**, 423–441.

Leff, J. P., Kuipers, L., Berkowitz, R., Eberlein-Fries, R. & Sturgeon, D. (1982). A controlled trial of social intervention in schizophrenic families. *British Journal of Psychiatry*, **141**, 121–134.

Leff, J. P. & Vaughn, C. (1985). *Expressed Emotion in Families*. New York: Guilford.

Leff, J., Berkowitz, R., Shavit, N., Strachan, A., Glass, I. & Vaughn, C. (1989). A trial of family therapy v. a relatives' group for schizophrenia. *British Journal of Psychiatry*, **154**, 58–66.

Leff, J., Berkowitz, R., Shavit, N., Strachan, A., Glass, I. & Vaughn, C. (1990). A trial of family therapy versus a relatives' group for schizophrenia: A two year follow-up. *British Journal of Psychiatry*, **157**, 571–577.

Llovet, J. M. (1991). Emocio expresada familiar i clinica de la esquizofrenia. Symposium on Expressed Emotion in Latin based languages. Barcelona, Spain.

MacCarthy, B., Kuipers, L., Hurry, J., Harper, R. & Lesage, A. (1989*a*). Evaluation of counselling for relatives of the long term adult mentally ill. *British Journal of Psychiatry*, **154**, 768–775.

MacCarthy, B., Lesage, A., Brewin, C. R., Brugha, T. S., Mangen, S. & Wing, J. K. (1989*b*). Needs for care among the relatives of long term users of day care. *Psychological Medicine*, **19**, 725–736.

Magana, A. B., Goldstein, M. J., Karno, M., Miklowitz, D. J., Jenkins, J. & Falloon, I. R. H. (1986). A brief method for assessing EE in relatives of psychiatric patients. *Psychiatry Research*, **2**, 203–212.

Marks, N. M., Wieck, A., Seymour, A., Checkley, S. A. & Kumar, R. (in press). Women whose mental illness occurs after childbirth and partners' level of EE during later pregnancy. *British Journal of Psychiatry*.

Mavreas, V. G., Tomaras, V., Karydi, V., Economon, M. & Stefanis, C. (1992). Expressed Emotion in families of chronic schizophrenics and its association with clinical measures. *Social Psychiatry and Psychiatric Epidemiology*, **27**, 4–9.

McCreadie, R. G., Phillips, K., Harvey, J. A., Waldron, G., Stewart, M. & Baird, D. (1991). The Nithsdale Schizophrenia Surveys VIII. Do relatives want family intervention and does it help? *British Journal of Psychiatry*, **158**, 110–113.

Montero, I., Gomez-Beneyto, M., Ruizie Puche, E. & Adam, A. (1992). The influence of family Expressed Emotion on the course of schizophrenia in a sample of Spanish patients: A two year follow-up study. Personal communication.

Moore, E., Ball, R. A. & Kuipers, L. (1992*a*). Expressed Emotion in staff working with the long-term adult mentally ill. *British Journal of Psychiatry* (in press).

Moore, E., Kuipers, L. & Ball, R. (1992*b*). Staff patient relationships in the case of the long-term mentally ill: A content analysis of EE interviews. *Social Psychiatry and Psychiatric Epidemiology*, **27**, 28–34.

Mozny, P. & Votypkova, P. (1992). Expressed Emotion, relapse rate and utilisation of psychiatric inpatient care in schizophrenia: A study from Czechoslovakia. *Social Psychiatry and Psychiatric Epidemiology*, **27**, 174–179.

Ochs, E. (1986). Introduction. In B. Schieffelin & E. Ochs (Eds), *Language Socialisation Across Cultures*, pp. 1–13. Cambridge: Cambridge University Press.

Orhagen, T. & d'Elia, G. (1991). EE: A Swedish version of the CFI. *Acta Psychiatrica Scandinavica*, **84**, 466–474.

Orhagen, T., d'Elia, G. & Gustafsson, P. (1992). Psycho-education and EE. Personal communication.

Peter, H. & Hand, P. (1988). Patterns of patient spouse interaction in agoraphobics: Assessment by CFI and impact on self-exposure treatment. In I. Hand & H. Wittchen (Eds), *Panic and Phobias 2: Treatment and Variables Affecting Course and Outcome,* pp. 240–251. Berlin: Springer-Verlag.

Priebe, S., Wildgrube, C. & Muller-Oerlinghausen, B. (1989). Lithium prophylaxis and Expressed Emotion. *British Journal of Psychiatry*, **154**, 396–399.

Priebe, S., Wildgrube, C. & Muller-Oerlinghausen, B. (1992*a*). Expressed Emotion and lithium prophylaxis: A follow-up study. Personal communication.

Priebe, S., Kuppers, A. J. & Sinning, U. (1992*b*). Expressed Emotion and coronary heart disease. Personal communication.

Pumar, B., Espina, A., Yerbe, A., Santos, A., Carcia, E. & Bel, A. (1991). Estudio correlacional entre la actitud de los padres (emocion expresada) hacia el hijo con patalogic psiquica (esquizofrenia y toxicomania) y la percepcion de los hijos de la conducta de sus padres. Symposium on Expressed Emotion in Latin based languages. Barcelona, Spain.

Rostworowska, M., Barbaro, B. & Maskowski, J. (1989). The influence of EE on the course of schizophrenia – Polish replications. Paper presented to XIX Congress of Behaviour Therapy, Vienna, Austria.

Sensky, T., Stevenson, K., Magrill, L. & Petty, R. (1991). Family Expressed Emotion in non-psychiatric illness: Adaptation of the Camberwell Family Interview to the families of adolescents with diabetes. *International Journal of Methods in Psychiatric Research*, **1**, 39–51.

Smith, J., Birchwood, M., Cochrane, R. & George, S. (1992). The needs of high and low Expressed Emotion families: A normative approach. *Social Psychiatry and Psychiatric Epidemiology*, (in press).

Stirling, J., Tantam, D., Thomas, P., Newby, D. & Montague, L. (1991). EE and early onset schizophrenia: A one year follow-up. *Psychological Medicine*, **21**, 675–685.

Szmukler, G. I., Eisler, I., Russell, G. F. M. & Dare, C. (1985). Anorexia nervosa, parental EE and dropping out of treatment. *British Journal of Psychiatry*, **147**, 265–271.

Tarrier, N. (1989). Electrodermal activity, EE and outcome in schizophrenia. *British Journal of Psychiatry*, Supplement **5**, 51–56.

Tarrier, N., Barrowclough, C., Porceddu, K. & Watts, S. (1988*a*). The assessment of psycho-physiological reactivity to the Expressed Emotion of the relatives of schizophrenic patients. *British Journal of Psychiatry*, **152**, 618–624.

Tarrier, N., Barrowclough, C., Vaughn, C., Bamrah, J. S., Porceddu, K., Watts, S. & Freeman, H. (1988*b*). The community management of schizophrenia: A controlled trial of a behavioural intervention with families to reduce relapse. *British Journal of Psychiatry*, **153**, 532–542.

Tarrier, N., Barrowclough, C., Vaughn, C., Bamrah, J. S., Porceddu, K., Watts, S. & Freeman, H. (1989). Community management of schizophrenia in a two year follow-up of a behavioural intervention with families. *British Journal of Psychiatry*, **154**, 625–628.

Van Furth, E. (1991). Parental Expressed Emotion and eating disorders. Unpublished Ph.D. thesis. Utrecht University, The Netherlands.

Vaughan, K., Doyle, M., McConathy, N. Blaszczynski, A., Fox, A. & Tarrier, N. (1992). The relationship between relatives' EE and schizophrenic relapse: An Australian replication. *Social Psychiatry and Psychiatric Epidemiology*, **27**, 10–15.

Vaughn, C. (1992). Inflammatory bowel syndrome and EE. Personal communication.

Vaughn, C. & Leff, J. (1976). The measurement of EE in the Families of Psychiatric Patients. *British Journal of Social and Clinical Psychology*, **15**, 157–165.

Watts, S. (1988). A descriptive investigation of the incidence of high EE in staff working with schizophrenic patients in a hospital setting. Unpublished dissertation for diploma in clinical psychology. British Psychological Society.

Wykes, T. (1982). A hostel ward for new long-stay patients. In Wing J. K. (Ed), Long-term community care. *Psychological Medicine Monograph Supplement* **2**, 59–97.

British Journal of Clinical Psychology (1992), **31**, 445–457   *Printed in Great Britain*

Social support and stress: The role of social comparison and social exchange processes

Bram P. Buunk* and **Vera Hoorens**

Department of Psychology, University of Groningen, Grote Kruisstraat 2/1, 9712 TS Groningen, The Netherlands

This paper first presents four different conceptualizations of social support: social integration, satisfying relationships, perceived helpfulness and enacted support. Then, classic and contemporary social comparison theory and social exchange theory are analysed as they are two theoretical perspectives that are particularly useful in understanding social support. These perspectives are employed to explain three seemingly paradoxical phenomena in the domain of social support: (1) the fact that support sometimes has negative effects; (2) the fact that the occurrence of stress itself can sometimes decrease the availability of support resources; and (3) the phenomenon that people believe that they give more support than they receive, and that there is more support available for them than for others.

Central to contemporary health psychology is the assumption that social support from significant others is of major importance in coping with important life-events, and that social support can reduce or eliminate the adverse consequences of these events upon health or well-being (for reviews see for instance, Cohen & Wills, 1985; Coyne & Downey, 1991; Sarason, Sarason & Pierce, 1990). However, findings on the role of support in alleviating stress are sometimes contradictory and difficult to interpret. In our view, this is largely due to a lack of attention given to the role of interpersonal processes and the mechanisms by which social support achieves its effects. In the present paper, a conceptual clarification of social support is presented and two theoretical perspectives are discussed that are particularly useful in understanding social support, i.e. social comparison theory and social exchange theory. These perspectives will then be employed to explain three seemingly paradoxical phenomena in the domain of social support: (1) the fact that support sometimes has negative effects: in some cases, social support appears to increase the impact stress has on well-being instead of reducing that effect; (2) the fact that the occurrence of stress itself can sometimes decrease the availability of support resources: remarkably, those under stress often perceive a deterioration of relationships and social support; and (3) the phenomenon that people believe that they give more support than they receive, and that there is more support available for them than for others, thus the existence of an egocentric bias in 'support bookkeeping'.

---

* Requests for reprints.

Social support: A conceptual clarification

Social support is embedded in ongoing social interactions that are part of an everchanging network of social relationships. While a sharp and generally accepted definition of social support as distinct from other types of social interaction is hard to make, it is possible to present a taxonomy of perspectives on social support that provides a useful tool in ordering its effects, and in identifying the social psychological processes involved. In a review of the occupational stress literature, Buunk (1990) made a distinction between four different conceptualizations of social support. First, from a sociological perspective, social support has primarily been viewed in terms of the number and strength of the connections of the individual to others in his or her social environment – in other words, the degree of one's social integration or the size and structure of one's social network. According to Rook (1984), social integration may promote health, among other things, by providing stable and rewarding roles, by promoting healthy behaviour, by deterring the person from ill-advised behaviour, and by maintaining stable functioning during periods of rapid change. A second perspective on social support has been provided by authors who equate social support with the availability of satisfying relationships characterized by love, intimacy, trust or esteem. For instance, Cutrona & Russell (1990) have shown that certain provisions of relationships, including attachment and reassurance of worth, can act as buffers against stress. In the third perspective, the perceived helpfulness view, social support constitutes the appraisal that, under stressful circumstances, others can be relied upon for advice, information and empathic understanding, guidance and support. In this context, there is some evidence for the assumption that the mere perception that one can turn to someone for help already reduces stress (Sarason & Sarason, 1986). Finally, for some authors the concept of social support refers primarily to the actual receiving of supportive acts from others once a stressful situation has come into existence. While the foregoing perspectives assume a certain preventive function of support against stress, this perspective focuses upon the curative function of actual help when a person is under stress (cf. Barrera, 1986). Although all these conceptualizations may be important for understanding the role of interpersonal relationships in reducing stress, the four levels may bear different relationships to health and well-being. For example, as Barrera (1986) has suggested, exposure to stress may trigger the enactment of supportive behaviours by others, thus leading to positive correlations between stress and enacted support. However, at the same time a high degree of perceived support may be negatively correlated with stress.

Social comparison, social exchange and social support

Social comparison theory

Although this is not always acknowledged within social psychology, research on social support in fact dates back to the early experiments of Schachter (1959) on the relationship between fear and affiliation. Schachter showed that fear due to the prospect of having to undergo an electric shock evoked in most subjects the desire to wait with someone else, but only with individuals in the same situation. According to Schachter, individuals under stress seek out others for reasons of self-evaluation, to assess the appropriateness of their own reactions. Later research has qualified Schachter's original findings by showing that the tendency to seek out the company of others decreases under many stressful situations, for instance when one is confronted with embarrassing circumstances. In a well-known experiment, Sarnoff & Zimbardo (1961) demonstrated that anxiety (caused by the prospect of having to suck bottles and other infantile objects), as opposed to fear, led to decreased affiliation. Teichman (1973) showed that fear of social rejection was the predominant reason for wanting to wait alone when embarrassed. Another condition that has been shown to keep people from making affiliations is the presence of strong emotions. For instance, in an early study among men who were cleaning up the site of an airplane crash in which 82 people were killed, Latané & Wheeler (1966) found that among the men who did the most stressful work, i.e. the searching of bodies and body parts, the more emotional men had less desire to talk to others and to write home than the less emotional men.

Not only are others avoided in embarrassing circumstances, there is also evidence that the presence of companions may increase stress reactions in such circumstances. For example, in a study by Glass, Gordon & Henchy (1970), subjects watched a film depicting an aboriginal puberty rite involving mutilation of the genitals of adolescent boys. In contrast to the theoretical expectations, it was found that the presence of a friend during the film led to a higher skin conductance than seeing the film alone or with strangers present. This finding can be interpreted by assuming that the film evokes an embarrassing type of stress, since it may stimulate repressed motives, such as castration anxiety and homosexuality, and that this stress is augmented by the fact that a friend is present. This suggests that under such conditions social support may have a negative effect.

More recent research has focused primarily upon the role of self-enhancement in stressful situations. Wills (1981) suggested that when individuals are confronted with a threat, they engage in downward comparisons with less competent others in an attempt to restore the way they feel about themselves. Various studies have indeed indicated that information about others worse off can lead to mood improvement (Gibbons, 1986; Testa & Major, 1990), and that when confronted with serious diseases such as arthritis (Affleck & Tennen, 1991) and cancer (Wood, Taylor & Lichtman, 1985), individuals tend to compare themselves with others who are worse off, and to perceive themselves as better off than most others facing the same or a similar stressor (Buunk, Collins, Van Yperen, Taylor & Pakof, 1990; Taylor, Buunk & Aspinwall, 1990).

While it seems evident that individuals do indeed tend to compare themselves with others who are less well off, it has become more and more clear that this preference does not extend to affiliative activity. In fact, as early as 1963, Rabbie showed that the high fear person was avoided in all conditions of the experiment that he conducted in the Schachter (1959) paradigm. Low fear subjects preferred a low fear companion, moderate fear subjects a moderate companion, but the high fear subjects also preferred a moderate fear companion. More recently, in a study of Molleman, Pruyn & van Knippenberg (1986), cancer patients indicated a preference for affiliation with others who were similarly or better off. Buunk, Van Yperen, Taylor

& Collins (1991) found that people in stressful marriages preferred to talk relatively more often with others who had better marriages, while those with happy marriages in general indicated a preference for interaction with others who were as happy as they were. Taylor & Lobel (1989) have interpreted such findings by arguing that individuals under stress are faced with two major coping tasks: regulating their emotions and obtaining relevant problem solving information. The first of these needs is best addressed through the use of downward, self-enhancing comparisons, while the latter requires contact with people who are better off. Thus, such upward affiliation may serve the motive of self-improvement. It may provide a person with valuable information for potential long-term survival and successful coping, and it may enhance the person's self-efficacy. It must be noted that while this model can predict upward affiliative preferences under stress, it cannot explain the preference for people in a similar situation found by Molleman *et al.* (1986).

Social exchange theory

Social exchange theory constitutes a second line of research within social psychology that may have important implications for social support and stress (for a discussion of exchange theory, see Burgess & Huston, 1979). In equity theory, the most influential social exchange theory, interpersonal relationships are viewed as consisting of an exchange of benefits governed by a norm of equity. In other words, the members in an exchange relation assume that a benefit is given with the expectation of receiving a benefit in return, and the very receipt of it incurs a debt or an obligation to return a similar or at least a comparable benefit. It is predicted that any disturbance of this expected reciprocity, either in the form of not being able to return benefits or not receiving benefits in return from others, will lead to negative affective reactions (Walster, Walster & Berscheid, 1978). Indeed, experimental research on the recipients' reactions to help suggests that helping actions may backfire and trigger negative feelings when people are not able or willing to reciprocate the helping behaviour, or when they receive a more favourable rate of outcomes than the person giving help (Hatfield & Sprecher, 1983). Inequity will especially feature when the aid is voluntary and deliberate, and when the person giving help is not supposed to receive any extrinsic gains from helping.

An important factor influencing the importance of equity considerations is the type of relationship. Equity seems to be especially important in exchange relationships such as business relationships, where reciprocity is expected and required, and to a lesser extent in communal relationships such as those between intimates (Mills & Clark, 1982). Nevertheless, while direct reciprocity seems not to be perceived as characteristic of intimate relationships, a large number of studies have shown the importance of a global perception of equity for satisfaction in personal relationships (e.g. Hatfield, Traupmann, Sprecher, Utne & Hay, 1984; Van Yperen & Buunk, 1990). Remarkably, although helping relationships have been analysed from the perspective of equity theory (Hatfield & Sprecher, 1983), it was not until recently that this theory was applied to the giving and receiving of social support. A few studies have examined reciprocity and equity with respect to social support within ongoing relationships. For example, Antonucci & Jackson (1990) discovered that people with disabilities attempted to maintain reciprocal supportive relationships. Roberto & Scott (1986) found less distress among older adults who perceived their relationship with their best friend as equitable. Rook (1987) suggested that giving more to a relationship than one receives leads to feelings of unfairness and resentment, whereas receiving more than one gives leads to feelings of guilt and shame. Her study of elderly widowed women showed that there was more reciprocity in relationships with friends than with adult children, and that receiving either more or less benefits in exchanges with members of the social network was associated with feelings of loneliness.

Social support: Three paradoxes

The theoretical perspectives outlined above can help explain the three paradoxes mentioned earlier that are either puzzling from a naïve perspective on social support, or that throw a surprising light on some of its implicitly assumed characteristics.

Negative effects of social support

The assumed beneficial effects of social support have often been divided into two types: direct and buffer effects. *Direct* effects encompass the general positive influence of social support, regardless of whether someone experiences special stress or not. A *buffer* effect refers to the fact that a high level of social support protects the individual against the negative consequences of stressors once these have arisen (Cohen & Wills, 1985). One of the puzzling findings in the domain of social support concerns the existence of negative direct as well as buffer effects (Barrera, 1986). For example, in a study of nurses, Kaufman & Beehr (1986) found that all the significant buffer effects turned out to be the opposite of their expectations: the relationship between sources of stress and stress reactions appeared to be higher among individuals who had access to strong social support systems than among individuals who lacked these systems. Winnubst, Marcelissen & Kleber (1982) found that people who had a high responsibility for others at work became more depressed when their colleagues and superiors were more supportive. In a study carried out by Hobfoll & London (1986) among Israeli women whose loved ones were mobilized in the 1982 Israel–Lebanon war, social support appeared to be related to greater psychological distress. In a study on occupational stress among nearly 2000 employees, Buunk, Janssen & Van Yperen (1989) noted so-called boomerang effects. For example, in some cases social support aggravated the stress reactions or did not affect them at all in work units characterized by a high degree of role conflict, while, at the same time, social support reduced stress reactions in units with a low degree of role conflict. In other words, support seemed to aggravate instead of alleviate stress.

While positive relations between stress and support may indicate that those under stress seek out help more often (Buunk & Verhoeven, 1991), in some cases social support does appear to increase the impact that stress has on well-being instead of reducing that effect. For various reasons, this seems quite understandable from a social comparison point of view. First, as indicated above (especially when a stress situation implies strong emotions, embarrassing experiences, or experiences that may evoke social disapproval), affiliation with others may aggravate stress (e.g. Friedman, 1981). Second, social comparison processes may cause stress by changing existing attitudes towards potentially stressful situations. For instance, on the basis of research on group polarization, it has been shown that when people engage in a discussion of potential problems occurring in a shared situation, and there is a predominantly negative view of these problems, they will develop an even more pronounced negative view after the discussion (Moscovici, 1985; see also Hobfoll & London, 1986). Furthermore, social comparison may have a *direct* influence upon reactions to specific stressors when other people exhibit particular responses that later become imitated by any newcomers to the group as they have been led to believe that such behaviour is quite normal in the given situation. Some experimental evidence relating to this issue is now beginning to emerge. Costanza, Derlega & Winstead (1988) examined the effect of various conversational topics among same-sex friends in anticipation of a stressful event (guiding a tarantula spider through a maze). Subjects who had been instructed to talk about their fears, feelings and anxieties experienced more negative affect, and kept the spider at a greater distance than subjects who had been instructed to engage in problem solving conversation. This last type of interaction is apparently more effective than emotional support when confronted with a fear arousing situation (see also Winstead & Derlega, 1991).

A high degree of support within a work unit may even foster the development of an intense phenomenon such as professional burnout among human service workers through social comparison and subsequent 'contagion' of stress reactions (e.g. Miller, Stiff & Ellis, 1988). However, social comparison theory would predict that not all individuals are affected to the same degree by the symptoms they perceive in others; those with a particularly strong need for social comparison would be sensitive to the perception of burnout symptoms in others. This is precisely what the data from a study of nurses suggest (Buunk & Schaufeli, in press). Nurses who had a need to learn more about others in a similar situation expressed a higher level of emotional exhaustion when they perceived that many of their colleagues showed burnout symptoms.

As suggested above, a lack of reciprocity in supportive interactions may also contribute to the negative effects of social support. Reciprocity may be more important in so-called exchange relationships, where something is expected in return for the support that is given, and where support may create feelings of indebtedness on the part of the recipient (Mills & Clark, 1982). At work, many relationships will be exchange relationships and negative effects of support that cannot be reciprocated may therefore be expected to be particularly strong in the context of support and stress at work (Buunk, 1990). Moreover, as suggested by Buunk & Verhoeven (1991), many people in professional relationships may be more sensitive to feelings of superiority or inferiority which are implied by giving or receiving social support.

Despite the claims of equity theorists, there is increasing evidence that lack of reciprocity with respect to support does not affect all people to the same degree. In a number of studies, Buunk and his colleagues have shown that the personality of the individuals concerned is crucial in determining the importance of equity and reciprocity for people's relationship satisfaction (Buunk & Van Yperen, 1991; Van Yperen & Buunk, 1991; Van Yperen, Buunk & Schaufeli, 1992). Two traits are considered of particular relevance in this respect: *exchange orientation* (Milardo & Murstein, 1979), the disposition to be strongly oriented to direct reciprocity, and *communal orientation* (Clark, Ouellette, Powell & Milberg, 1987), the desire to give and receive benefits in response to the needs of, or concern for, others. Applying these concepts on the exchange of social support in an occupational setting, Buunk, Jans, Doosje & Hopstaken (1991) found only among railway employees high in exchange orientation or low in communal orientation was lack of reciprocity related to negative affect. The fact that the personality of the individuals concerned seems to be related to the effects of unreciprocal support may partially explain the inconsistent findings on the effects of support in studies in which individual difference factors have not been taken into account.

Finally, it should be noted that equity theory would predict different effects of social support depending on how support is operationalized. Indeed, social support viewed as social integration or the quality of social relationships implies at least the possibility of reciprocity, whereas a definition of social support in terms of the perceived helpfulness of others or the actual help received from them, implies more an individual in need of help and one or more other(s) willing or not to provide support. Therefore, research is more likely to yield negative effects of social support when support is operationalized in one of the latter two ways than when it is measured in one of the former two ways. Support for this contention can be derived from the study by Buunk & Verhoeven (1991) among police officers, in which it was found that rewarding social interactions on duty were accompanied by less negative emotions at the end of the day, whereas receiving a high level of intimate or instrumental help during the work day was accompanied by more negative affect afterwards.

In addition to the factors discussed here, other factors may also contribute to negative effects of support. These include the undermining of feelings of competence and control (Coates, Renzaglia & Embree, 1983) and threats to self-esteem, such as when help conflicts with values of self-reliance and independence (Fisher, Nadler & Witcher-Alagna, 1982). Furthermore, many probably well-intended support attempts seem to fail because people providing support often seem to say the wrong things at the wrong times (e.g. Lehman & Hemphill, 1990). Nevertheless, social comparison and social exchange theory seem to offer an especially fruitful foundation for understanding the negative effects of support.

Deterioration of relationships and social support under stress

As a second paradox, it is apparent from a number of studies that the occurrence of stressors may sometimes negatively influence the amount of social support that is perceived to be available to an individual, thus reducing this important factor for coping just when it is needed the most. In a longitudinal study carried out by Marcelissen, Buunk, Winnubst & De Wolff (1988) amongst a large group of Dutch white- and blue-collar employees, the causal relations between support and stress could be examined. It was found that for the lower level employees, affective complaints and worry influenced social support from co-workers negatively: employees who showed these strains to a high degree received less support from their colleagues than their more fortunate peers. For the higher occupational group a similar pattern of results was obtained with regard to affective strains and regular health complaints. In other words, perceived support from colleagues seemed to be negatively influenced by the strains that people experience.

There are various processes that may lead to a negative effect of stress upon perceived support. First, stress in the form of negative affect may make others look less attractive, as can be concluded from research on interpersonal attraction. Research by Byrne and his colleagues (Byrne, 1971, pp. 359) has shown that people in whom a negative mood was induced (through a film, or high temperature, for example) perceive others less positively than people in whom a positive mood is induced. Second, stressful circumstances at work may decrease actual affiliation with others out of fear of looking incompetent (e.g. Teichman, 1973). Indeed, Buunk & Schaufeli (in press) showed that, although individuals with a high degree of occupational stress had a relatively high need for affiliation, i.e. a desire to talk with others about problems at work, they tended at the same time to avoid the company of their colleagues. Remarkably, the desire to affiliate under stress was more manifest among those with high self-esteem. This result can be understood if it is assumed that people who are high in self-esteem are relatively less concerned about being temporarily competent in comparison with another, than those with a low level of self-esteem.

Stress can also lead to decreased support because others turn away from people under stress. Indeed, many stressful situations, particularly stigmatizing or strongly traumatizing events, seem to affect social relationships in a negative way, such as by alienating others, by depleting their resources or even by causing caregiver burnout. Such circumstances may reduce the willingness or ability of others to provide support (Barrera, 1986; Cohen-Silver, Wortman & Crofton, 1990; Coyne, Ellard & Smith, 1990; Hobfoll & Parris-Stephens, 1990; Shinn, Lehman & Wong, 1984). There is also considerable evidence that interacting with depressed individuals is seen to be aversive (e.g. Coyne, 1976). These findings are in line with the literature on social comparison that shows that individuals under stress are often avoided by others, a process through which people who are under most stress may end up isolated (e.g. Rabbie, 1963). Indeed, people seem to prefer the company of others who are equally well off or better off, as this type of interaction provides them with pleasant interactions and the necessary information further to improve their own situation. As a consequence, peers of a stressed person may prefer to turn to even better-off others instead of investing time and effort in helping their troubled peer. In the study by Buunk & Schaufeli (in press) on occupational stress and burnout, there was a general preference for upward affiliation. About half of the subjects, whether under stress or not, expressed a preference for affiliation with others who were more competent in their work. In the remaining sample, all indicated a preference for others equally competent as themselves, and nobody was interested in affiliation with others less competent. Interestingly, these data suggest that affiliation preferences may often not be satisfied as people who prefer upward affiliation will rarely meet someone who wants to talk to them. As there is some evidence, mentioned before, that people under stress may prefer contacts with others who are better off (Buunk et al., 1991), they may be particularly frustrated in their attempts to obtain the support they desire.

From the perspective of equity theory, individuals under stress may actively avoid others in order not to find themselves in the uneven position of having to accept help without knowing when and how they will be able to restore equity. In turn, both lay people and professional helpers may find it difficult to maintain good relationships with individuals under stress because of the extreme or chronic one-sided nature of the interaction. One of the causes of burnout in human service professions is the lack of rewarding interactions experienced by caregivers in their relation with stressed clients (Van Yperen, Buunk & Schaufeli, 1992). Evidence from the psychiatric literature suggests that psychiatric patients tend to maintain asymmetrical helping relationships, failing to reciprocate the support they receive from others (Gottlieb, 1985). As Gottlieb has noted, such an imbalance '...makes interaction less satisfying for both parties, because the helper is drained and the recipient feels uncomfortably indebted, suffering also a decline in good feelings about him/herself' (p. 430).

Giving more support than one receives and receiving more support than others

Intuitively, it is reasonable to assume that some people receive more support than others, due to factors such as the special strains put upon them by the specific nature of their life circumstances, by individual variations in vulnerability to stress, or to a combination of these factors. As a consequence, some people may give more support to others than they receive themselves, while other people may receive more support than they give. Thus, on a group level the average amount of support given and support received should be balanced. However, there is some evidence for an egocentric bias in 'support bookkeeping'. In two studies on occupational stress by Buunk *et al.* (1992), a group of psychiatric nurses and a group of employees of the Dutch railway company were asked to assess whether they provided more, as much, or less support to both their superior and their colleagues as they received themselves from these people. Most participants perceived reciprocity in both their relationships with their superior and their colleagues. Of the remaining participants, however, a majority reported that they gave more support to their co-workers than they received from them. For the railway employees, this difference was even found in their relationship with their superior.

In apparent contrast to these findings, when individuals compare the social support they receive to the social support other people receive from others, they relatively overestimate the degree to which they enjoy support from other people. For instance, Affleck & Tennen (1991) found that women with fertility problems believed that they could rely on more social support than other women in the same situation. Brinthaupt, Moreland & Levine (1991) found that freshmen at university expected to receive more benefits and less costs from their prospective membership of several student groups than other students joining the same group. In a large quality of life survey by Campbell, Converse & Rodgers (1976), 38 per cent of the respondents claimed that they had more close friends to lean on in times of stress than the average person, while only half that number (19 per cent) said they had less than the average number of such friends.

The simultaneously existing evidence for an intra-individual give-and-get bias (people believe that they give more support than they get) and for an inter-individual get-and-get bias (people believe that more support is available to themselves than to

Bram P. Buunk and Vera Hoorens

others) may seem rather puzzling when social support is studied in isolation. However, it becomes easily understandable when the phenomenon is linked to social comparison processes. There is now ample evidence for what we would like to call 'illusory superiority': the widespread belief that one's own future will be better, and that one's own skills, abilities, personality traits and life circumstances are better than those of other people (e.g. Brown, 1986; Weinstein, 1980). This phenomenon has been shown in such diverse domains as the assessment and prediction of academic success (e.g. Alloy & Ahrens, 1987) and estimation of the likelihood of encountering marital problems leading to divorce (e.g. Perloff & Fetzer, 1986). However, it has been studied most intensively in the context of health problems. Several researchers have found that people believe they are at lower risk than their peers of getting coronary or venereal diseases, lung cancer and many other health problems (Weinstein, 1980, 1982). Realizing the ubiquitous nature of this phenomenon, it becomes clear why people simultaneously believe that they give more support than they get and that they get more support than other people. Indeed, both giving more than one takes, and getting more of a resource which is assumed to be beneficial, are an indication of one's own superiority.

Summary and conclusion

It was the contention of the present paper that the atheoretical nature of a large part of the social support literature leaves the domain with a number of puzzling findings which are difficult to incorporate in a general body of knowledge. Two theoretical perspectives – social comparison theory and social exchange theory – were suggested that may contribute to an integration of these and other findings and that may be fruitful in developing specific predictions of the effects of different types of social support in different situations and relationships and people's different personalities. The relevance of this approach was demonstrated in the context of three paradoxical phenomena, mostly illustrated with examples from our own research programme.

Of course, the present paper is not meant to state that only social comparison theory and social exchange are relevant in the context of social support research. As has been mentioned repeatedly, other theories and findings are equally relevant in clarifying the determinants and the effects of social support. Neither does the present article deny the positive direct and buffer effects of social support that are often obtained, nor is it meant to suggest that social support is generally not available in situations where it is highly desirable and to individuals who are in special need of it. The point made here is that the beneficial effects and the automatic presence of social support should not be taken for granted. In addition, it was argued that the availability and the effects of support become more understandable in the light of well-established social-psychological theories. From this point of view, it is worthwhile to work towards a further integration of social-psychological theorizing into the domain of social support in order to identify interventions that maximize the beneficial effects of support as well as its availability in those situations where it is needed and for those who need it.

References

Affleck, G. & Tennen, H. (1991). Social comparison and coping with serious medical problems. In J. Suls & T. A. Wills (Eds), *Social Comparison. Contemporary Theory and Research*. Hillsdale, NJ: Erlbaum.

Alloy, L. B. & Ahrens, A. H. (1987). Depression and pessimism for the future: Biased use of statistically relevant information in predictions for self and others. *Journal of Personality and Social Psychology*, **52**, 366–378.

Antonucci, T. C. & Jackson, J. S. (1990). The role of reciprocity in social support. In B. R. Sarason, I. G. Sarason & G. R. Pierce (Eds), *Social Support: An Interactional View*. New York: Wiley.

Barrera, M. (1986). Distinction between social support concepts, measures and models. *American Journal of Community Psychology*, **14**, 413–445.

Brinthaupt, T. M., Moreland, R. L. & Levine, J. M. (1991). Sources of optimism among prospective group members. *Personality and Social Psychology Bulletin*, **17**, 36–43.

Brown, J. D. (1986). Evaluations of self and others: Self-enhancement biases in social judgments. *Social Cognition*, **4**, 353–376.

Burgess, R. L. & Huston, T. L. (Eds) (1979). *Social Exchange in Developing Relationships*. New York: Academic Press.

Buunk, B. P. (1990). Affiliation and helping interactions within organizations: A critical analysis of the role of social support with regard to occupational stress. In W. Stroebe & M. Hewstone (Eds), *European Review of Social Psychology*, vol. 1, pp. 293–322. Chichester: Wiley.

Buunk, B., Collins, R., Van Yperen, N. W., Taylor, S. E. & Dakof, G. (1990). Upward and downward comparisons: Either direction has its ups and downs. *Journal of Personality and Social Psychology*, **59**, 1238–1249.

Buunk, B. P., Jans, L. G. J. M., Doosje, B. J. & Hopstaken, L. E. M. (1991). Reciprocity, social support, and stress at work: The role of exchange orientation and communal orientation. Manuscript under review.

Buunk, B. P., Janssen, P. P. M. & Van Yperen, N. W. (1989). Stress and affiliation reconsidered: The effects of social support in stressful and non-stressful work units. *Social Behaviour*, **4**, 155–171.

Buunk, B. P. & Schaufeli, W. B. (in press). Professional burnout: A perspective from social comparison theory. In W. B. Schaufeli, T. Marek & C. Maslach (Eds), *Professional Burnout: Recent Developments in Theory and Research*. New York: Hemisphere.

Buunk, B. P. & Van Yperen, N. W. (1991). Referential comparison, relational comparison, and exchange orientation: Their relation to marital satisfaction. *Personality and Social Psychology Bulletin*, **17**, 710–718.

Buunk, B. P., Van Yperen, N. W., Taylor, S. E. & Collins, R. L. (1991). Social comparison and the drive upward revisited: Affiliation as a response to marital stress. *European Journal of Social Psychology*, **21**, 529–549.

Buunk, B. P. & Verhoeven, K. (1991). Companionship and support at work: A microanalysis of the stress-reducing features of social interaction. *Basic and Applied Social Psychology*, **12**, 243–258.

Byrne, D. (1971). *The Attraction Paradigm*. New York: Academic Press.

Campbell, A., Converse, P. E. & Rodgers, W. L. (1976). *The Quality of American Life*. New York: Sage.

Clark, M. S., Ouellette, R., Powell, M. C. & Milberg, S. (1987). Recipient's mood, relationship type, and helping. *Journal of Personality and Social Psychology*, **53**, 93–103.

Coates, D., Renzaglia, G. J. & Embree, M. C. (1983). When helping backfires: Help and helplessness. In J. D. Fisher, A. Nadler & B. M. DePaulo (Eds), *New Directions in Helping Behavior*, vol. 1. New York, Academic Press.

Cohen, S. & Wills, T. A. (1985). Stress, social support and the buffering hypothesis. *Psychological Bulletin*, **98**, 310–357.

Cohen Silver, R., Wortman, C. B. & Crofton, C. (1990). The role of coping in support provision: The self-presentational dilemma of victims of life crises. In I. G. Sarason, B. R. Sarason & G. R. Pierce (Eds), *Social support: An Interactional View*, pp. 397–426. New York: Wiley.

Costanza, R. S., Derlega, V. J. & Winstead, B. A. (1988). Positive and negative forms of social support: Effects of conversational topics on coping with stress among same sex friends. *Journal of Experimental Social Psychology*, **24**, 182–193.

Coyne, J. C. (1976). Depression and the response of others. *Journal of Abnormal Psychology*, **85**, 186–193.

Coyne, J. C. & Downey, G. (1991). Social factors and psychopathology: Stress, social support and coping processes. *Annual Review of Psychology*, **42**, 401–429.

Coyne, J. C., Ellard, J. H. & Smith, D. A. F. (1990). Social support, interdependence, and the dilemmas of helping. In B. R. Sarason, I. G. Sarason & G. R. Pierce (Eds), *Social Support: An Interactional View*. New York. New York: Wiley.

Cutrona, C. & Russell, D. (1990). Type of social support and specific stress: Toward a theory of optimal matching. In B. R. Sarason, I. G. Sarason & G. R. Pierce (Eds), *Social Support: An Interactional View*. New York: Wiley.

Fisher, J. D., Nadler, A. & Witcher-Alagna, S. (1982). Recipient reactions to aid. *Psychological Bulletin*, **91**, 27–54.

Friedman, L. (1981). How affiliation affects stress in fear and anxiety situations. *Journal of Personality and Social Psychology*, **40**, 1102–1117.

Gibbons, F. X. (1986). Social comparison and depression: Company's effect on misery. *Journal of Personality and Social Psychology*, **51**, 140–148.

Glass, D. C., Gordon, A. & Henchy, T. (1970). The effects of social stimuli on psychophysiological reactivity to an aversive film. *Psychonomic Science*, **20**, 255–256.

Gottlieb, B. (1985). Theory into practice: Issues that surface in planning interventions which mobilize support. In I. G. Sarason & B. R. Sarason (eds), *Social Support: Theory, Research, and Applications*. Boston: Martinus Nijhoff.

Hatfield, E. & Sprecher, S. (1983). Equity theory and recipients' reactions to help. In J. D. Fisher, A. Nadler & B. M. DePaulo (Eds), *New Directions in Helping Behavior*, vol. 1. New York: Academic Press.

Hatfield, E., Traupmann, J., Sprecher, S., Utne, M. & Hay, J. (1984). Equity and intimate relations: Recent research. In W. Ickes (Ed.), *Compatible and Incompatible Relationships*, pp. 1–27. New York: Springer-Verlag.

Hobfoll, S. E. & London, P. (1986). The relationship of self-concept and social support to emotional distress among women during war. *Journal of Social and Clinical Psychology*, **4**, 189–202.

Hobfoll, S. E. & Parris-Stephens, M. A. (1990). Social support during extreme stress: Consequences and intervention. In B. R. Sarason, I. G. Sarason & G. R. Pierce (Eds), *Social Support: An Interactional View*. New York: Wiley.

Kaufman, G. M. & Beehr, T. A. (1986). Interactions between job stressors and social support: Some counterintuitive results. *Journal of Applied Psychology*, **71**, 522–526.

Latané, B. & Wheeler, L. (1966). Emotionality and reactions to disaster. *Journal of Experimental Psychology*. Supplement, **1**, 95–102.

Lehman, D. R. & Hemphill, K. J. (1990). Recipients' perceptions of support attempts and attributions for support attempts that fail. *Journal of Social and Personal Relationships*, **7**, 563–574.

Marcelissen, F. H. G., Buunk, B., Winnubst, J. A. M. & De Wolff, C. J. (1988). Social support and occupational stress: A causal analysis. *Social Science and Medicine*, **26**, 365–373.

Milardo, R. M. & Murstein, B. I. (1979). The implications of exchange-orientation on the dyadic functioning of heterosexual cohabitors. In M. Cook & G. Wilson (Eds), *Love and Attraction: An International Conference*. Oxford: Pergamon Press.

Miller, K. I., Stiff, J. B. & Ellis, B. H. (1988). Communication and empathy as precursors to burnout among human service workers. *Communication Monographs*, **55**, 250–265.

Mills, J. & Clark, M. (1982). Exchange and communal relationships. In L. Wheeler (Ed.), *Review of Personality and Social Psychology*, vol. 3. Beverly Hills, CA: Sage.

Molleman, E., Pruyn, J. & van Knippenberg, A. (1986). Social comparison processes among cancer patients. *British Journal of Social Psychology*, **25**, 1–13.

Moscovici, S. (1985). Social influence and conformity. In G. Lindzey & E. Aronson (Eds), *Handbook of Social Psychology*. New York: Random House.

Perloff, L. S. & Fetzer, B. K. (1986). Self–other judgments and perceived vulnerability to victimization. *Journal of Personality and Social Psychology*, **50**, 502–510.

Rabbie, J. M. (1963). Differential preference for companionship under threat. *Journal of Abnormal and Social Psychology*, **67**, 643–648.

Roberto, K. A. & Scott, J. P. (1986). Equity considerations in the friendships of older adults. *Journal of Gerontology*, **41**, 241–247.

Rook, K. (1984). Research on social support, loneliness and social isolation. In Ph. Shaver (Ed.), *Review of Personality and Social Psychology*, vol. 5. Beverly Hills, CA: Sage.

Rook, K. S. (1987). Reciprocity of social exchange and social satisfaction among older women. *Journal of Personality and Social Psychology*, **52**, 145–154.

Sarason, I. G. & Sarason, B. R. (Eds) (1986). Experimentally provided social support. *Journal of Personality and Social Psychology*, **50**, 1222–1225.

Sarason, B. R., Sarason, I. G. & Pierce, G. R. (Eds) (1990). *Social Support: An Interactional View*. New York: Wiley.

Sarnoff, I. & Zimbardo, P. G. (1961). Anxiety, fear, and social facilitation. *Journal of Abnormal and Social Psychology*, **62**, 597–605.

Schachter, S. (1959). *The Psychology of Affiliation*. Palo Alto, CA: Stanford University Press.

Shinn, M., Lehman, S. & Wong, N. W. (1984). Social interaction and social support. *Journal of Social Issues*, **40**, 55–76.

Taylor, S. E., Buunk, B. P. & Aspinwall, L. A. (1990). Social comparison, stress and coping. *Personality and Social Psychology Bulletin*, **16**, 74–89.

Taylor, S. E. & Lobel, M. (1989). Social comparison activity under threat: Downward evaluation and upward contacts. *Psychological Review*, **96**, 569–575.

Teichmann, Y. (1973). Emotional comparison and affiliation. *Journal of Experimental Social Psychology*, **9**, 591–605.

Testa, M. & Major, B. (1990). The impact of social comparison after failure: The moderating effects of perceived control. *Basic and Applied Social Psychology*, **11**, 205–218.

Van Yperen, N. W. & Buunk, B. P. (1990). A longitudinal study of equity and satisfaction in intimate relationships. *European Journal of Social Psychology*, **20**, 287–309.

Van Yperen, N. W. & Buunk, B. P. (1991). Equity theory, exchange orientation and communal orientation from a cross-national perspective. *Journal of Social Psychology*, **131**, 5–20.

Van Yperen, N. W., Buunk, B. P. & Schaufeli, W. B. (1992). Communal orientation and the burnout syndrome among nurses. *Journal of Applied Social Psychology*, **22**, 173–189.

Walster, E. G., Walster, W. & Berscheid, E. (1978). *Equity: Theory and Research*. Boston: Allyn & Bacon.

Weinstein, N. D. (1980). Unrealistic optimism about future life events. *Journal of Personality and Social Psychology*, **39**, 806–820.

Weinstein, N. D. (1982). Unrealistic optimism about susceptibility to health problems. *Journal of Behavioral Medicine*, **5**, 441–460.

Wills, T. A. (1981). Downward comparison principles in social psychology. *Psychological Bulletin*, **90**, 245–271.

Winnubst, J. A. M., Buunk, B. & Marcelissen, F. G. H. (1988). Social support and stress: Perspectives and processes. In S. Fisher & J. Reason (Eds), *Handbook of Life Stress, Cognition and Health*, pp. 511–530. New York: Wiley.

Winnubst, J. A. M., Marcelissen, F. G. H. & Kleber, R. J. (1982). Effects of social support in the stressor–strain relationship: A Dutch sample. *Social Science and Medicine*, **16**, 475–482.

Winstead, B. A. & Derlega, V. J. (1991). An experimental approach to studying social interaction and coping with stress among friends. In W. H. Jones & D. Perlman (Eds), *Advances in Personal Relationships*, vol. 2, pp. 107–132. London: Kingsley.

Wood, J. V., Taylor, S. E. & Lichtman, R. R. (1985). Social comparison in adjustment to breast cancer. *Journal of Personality and Social Psychology*, **49**, 1169 1183.

British Journal of Clinical Psychology (1992), **31**, 459–472   *Printed in Great Britain*

Conditioning of drug-induced immunomodulation in human volunteers: A European Collaborative Study

C. Kirschbaum
Department of Clinical and Physiological Psychology, University of Trier, Trier-Tarforst, Germany

L. Jabaaij*
Department of Clinical Immunology, University Hospital Utrecht, The Netherlands

A. Buske-Kirschbaum
Department of Clinical and Physiological Psychology, University of Trier, Trier-Tarforst, Germany

J. Hennig
Department of Differential and Diagnostic Psychology, University of Giessen, Germany

M. Blom
Department of Clinical Immunology, University Hospital Utrecht, The Netherlands

K. Dorst
University of Münster Medical School, Germany

J. Bauch
Institute for Arteriosclerosis Research, University of Münster, Germany

R. DiPauli and G. Schmitz
University of Münster Medical School, Germany

R. Ballieux
Department of Clinical Immunology, University Hospital Utrecht, The Netherlands

D. Hellhammer*
Department of Clinical and Physiological Psychology, University of Trier, Germany

Although several studies on conditioning of the immune system in animals have been published, no comparable data on human research have been available in the past. The present paper presents results of conditioning studies in volunteers performed in two research centres, namely the University of Trier (Germany) and the University of Utrecht (The Netherlands). After administration of a neutral

* Requests for reprints.

stimulus (conditioned stimulus: CS), subjects were injected with epinephrine (unconditioned stimulus) for three or four days (depending on study). Subcutaneous injection of epinephrine caused a rapid enhancement of the activity of natural killer cells (NKCA) in venous blood, which was chosen as the unconditioned response. On the test trial, when saline instead of epinephrine was injected, the Trier group found a conditional enhancement of NKCA. No changes in NKCA were found in the control subjects, who received saline injections on all days along with the CS. The Utrecht group tried to replicate these results using a slightly different design. After obtaining non-confirmative results, the Utrecht experimenters tried to parallel the experimental settings of the Trier group as closely as possible. However, once again they failed to replicate the results of the Trier group. Possible reasons for the different results obtained in the two research groups are discussed.

Several lines of evidence suggest bidirectional communications between the central nervous system (CNS), the endocrine system and the immune system. Specific receptors for hormones and neuropeptides have been found on leucocytes (Bost, 1988) and a widespread innervation of lymphoid tissues by sympathetic nerves has been revealed (for a review see Felten & Felten, 1991). On the other hand, monokines and lymphokines produced by activated cells of the immune system induce significant changes in central neuronal activity, which in effect are signals from the body's defence system to the brain (Berkenbosch, van Oers, del Rey, Tilders & Besedovsky, 1987; Blalock, 1984; Sapolsky, Rivier, Yamamoto, Plotsky & Vale, 1987).

Additionally, recent data suggest that immunomodulation can result from higher cortical processes, e.g. stress and learning. Among the multiple approaches to studying these complex interactions, the paradigm of classical conditioning has frequently been used. In animal models, immune suppression as well as immune enhancement of humoral and cellular immune parameters have been observed following classical conditioning (for reviews see Ader & Cohen, 1985, 1991). Furthermore, the impact of behavioural conditioning on the development and course of certain diseases like lupus erythematosus (Ader & Cohen, 1982) and tumour growth (Ghanta, Hiramoto, Solvason & Spector, 1985) has been shown in rodents. Despite growing evidence of conditioned immune responses in animals, no comparable data have been available in humans.

The present study examined the effect of a classical conditioning procedure on natural killer cell activity (NKCA) in healthy human subjects. NK cells are defined as a subpopulation of large granular lymphocytes that spontaneously kill certain tumour and virus infected cells. They appear to play a major role in imm-unosurveillance against neoplastic disease, fungi and certain viral infections (Herberman & Ortaldo, 1981). Like other substances such as polyinosinic-polycytidylic acid (poly I:C) or interferons, epinephrine has been shown to increase NKCA non-specifically. After injection of 0.2 mg epinephrine subcutaneously in healthy volunteers an elevation of NKCA within 15 minutes has been observed. After two hours NKCA is back to baseline levels (Tönnesen, Tönnesen & Christensen, 1984). In contrast to the use of poly I:C, which results in comparable NKCA responses, no significant side-effects have been reported for epinephrine (Crary *et al.*, 1983). Subcutaneous epinephrine injections with their rapid but short-lasting effect without harmful consequences could thus be well suited as unconditioned stimuli (US) in human conditioning studies with NKCA being the dependent measure. In this paper the results of a two-centre study (Trier in Germany, and Utrecht in The Netherlands) on conditioned modulation of NKCA and NK cell numbers in peripheral blood in human volunteers are reported. It was investigated whether repeated pairings of epinephrine injections (US) with a neutral/conditioned stimulus (CS) would yield enhanced NKCA as the conditioned response (CR) after CS re-exposure and placebo treatment on the conditioning test trial. Plasma epinephrine levels, the number of NK cells in the peripheral blood and salivary cortisol were measured in the Trier study to control for possible changes in NKCA as a result of altered blood flow or a consequence of stress responses. The Utrecht group concentrated on several experimental conditions which could induce changes in sensitivity of NK cells to epinephrine. In addition, the influence of monocytes in the *in vitro* assay of NKCA was examined. We report on conflicting results obtained in both centres despite considerable efforts to establish identical experimental and analytical conditions with close collaboration between the two research groups involved. The relevance of the findings will be discussed.

Methods

General design

Subjects arrived at the laboratory in the morning at the same time every day to control for possible circadian rhythm effects. Experiments were performed with two subjects together in one room. After insertion of an indwelling venous catheter, subjects rested for 30 min. Then the CS was administered to the subjects followed by a subcutaneous injection with epinephrine (experimental group) or saline (control group) in the upper arm (UCS). Blood was drawn before the administration of the CS (the baseline sample) and after injection with epinephrine (E) to determine the NKCA and the number of NK cells. This procedure was repeated on three or four consecutive days (depending on study). On the test trial both groups were injected with saline.

This is the general outline of the experimental set-up. The protocols of both groups differed slightly in some aspects as described below. Table 1 summarizes the most important differences in protocol between the two research groups.

Protocol Trier: Experimental design

Fourteen healthy adults (12 men, two women; mean age 26.5 years) were randomly assigned to either the experimental ($N = 7$) or the control ($N = 7$) group and treated for four consecutive days with the test trial on day 5. They were informed that they would be injected with an endogenous substance which causes no side-effects to evaluate its impact on immunological processes. Furthermore the investigators announced that after the final experimental day the volunteers would be completely informed about the precise nature of the substance. This strategy was chosen to avoid contamination of data due to anticipatory or placebo effects. Subjects arrived at the laboratory at 8 a.m. and rested for 20 min before an indwelling catheter was inserted which was kept open by a slowly dropping saline infusion. Then the volunteers rested for 30 min before the first blood sample was taken. Ten minutes later subjects were asked to press a sherbet sweet between their moistened lips for 10 s (CS). This caused a release of CO_2, resulting in a fizzing sensation. Subsequently, an injection with the UCS was administered. Twenty minutes after the injection the second blood sample was taken. Saliva samples were obtained employing the 'salivette' sampling device (Hellhammer, Kirschbaum & Belkien, 1987). Sampling was performed upon arrival at the laboratory (8.05 and 8.15 a.m.), following venepuncture (9.00 a.m.), before and after injection (9.10 and 9.30 a.m.), and at the end of each session, respectively.

Table 1. Differences in study protocols

	Trier	Utrecht	
	($N=12$ men, 2 women)	Expt I ($N = 6$ men)	Expt II ($N = 7$ men)
Arrival at laboratory	8.00 am	8.30 am	8.30 am
Administration CS and E	9.10 am	9.10 am	9.10 am
Groups	Experimental: E Control: saline	Experimental: E Control: saline	Experimental: E No control
CS	Sherbet sweet	Bitter drink	Sherbet sweet
No. acquisition trials	4 days	3 days	4 days
Blood taking	-10, 20 min	-10, 5, 45 min	-10, 5, 45 min
Knowledge of injection content	No	Yes	Yes
Analyses	NKCA (assay incl. monocytes), CD57+ cells, salivary cortisol, plasma E concentration	NKCA (monocytes removed), CD16+ cells	NKCA (with and without monocytes), CD16+ cells, *in vitro* stimulation with E

Note: E: epinephrine.

Immunologic analyses. On days 1 and 5, NKCA was measured using a standard [51]chromium release assay. Fifteen ml of heparinized venous blood were diluted with an equal volume of balanced salt solution (BSS) and layered on to 50 ml Ficoll-Hypaque (Pharmacia, Upsala, Sweden). Samples were centrifuged for 35 min at 400 g. Mononuclear cells were harvested from the interface, washed three times in BSS and subsequently counted under trypan blue exclusion; 2×10^6 target K562 cells were suspended in 100 μl BSS and incubated for 1 hour with 100 μCi $Na_2^{51}CrO_4$ at 37 °C and 5 per cent CO_2. After incubation, the labelled cells were washed three times in BSS and resuspended at a concentration of 10^5 cells per ml in Dulbecco's modified Eagles medium (DME). Mononuclear cells were co-cultured with labelled target cells at effector-target cell ratios of 100:1, 50:1, 25:1 and 12.5:1, respectively, for six hours at 37 °C and 5 per cent CO_2. Thereafter, 100 μl of cell-free supernatant was harvested from each well and radioactivity was measured in a gamma-counter for 1 min/sample. Spontaneous release was measured from the supernatants of K562 cells incubated without lymphoid cells, and the maximum release was obtained after adding 1 M NaOH to 10^4 targets. Cell lysis was calculated according to the formula NKCA % = ((exp. release − spont. release)/(max. release − spont. release)) × 100 %.

FACS analyses were performed in whole blood with the 'Simultest Immune Monitoring Kit' (Becton Dickinson) using the protocol as outlined by the manufacturer. The functionally significant subset of NK cells was identified with fluorescein isothiocyanate-labelled (FITC) Anti-Leu-7 antibodies (CD57); data analysis was performed with the CONSORT 30 software.

Hormone analyses. Plasma for the assessment of the catecholamine concentration was frozen at −40 degrees centigrade until assessment. Catecholamines were isolated from plasma using a solvent extraction procedure after complex formation of these compounds with diphenylboric acid. Epinephrine concentrations were determined by HPLC (column: 25 cm – Nucleosil 5C18 from Macherey & Nagel); mobile phase: 52.5 mM methane sulphonic acid; 29.6 mM phosphoric acid, 0.1 mM octanesulphonic acid, 0.1 mM EDTA, pH 2.1; flow rate: 1.0 ml/min) and electrochemical detection (detector potential against Ag/AgCl: 700 mV). The concentration of epinephrine was calculated measuring peak height. For further analytical detail refer to Bauch, Kelsch & Hauss (1986).

The saliva samples for cortisol assessment were frozen and thawed after sampling. Subsequently, devices were centrifuged at 3000 rpm for 2 min, resulting in a clear saliva of low viscosity. The samples were stored at −20 degrees centigrade until being assayed for salivary cortisol. Salivary cortisol was assayed with a slightly modified commercial radioimmunoassay (RIA) serum cortisol kit. The protocol of the 'Magic Cortisol' RIA (Ciba-Corning, Giessen, Germany) was modified as outlined elsewhere (Kirschbaum, Strasburger, Jammers & Hellhammer, 1989).

Data analysis. Student's *t*-tests for dependent and independent measures were performed to reveal statistical differences in natural killer cell activity, number of CD57+ cells, plasma epinephrine concentration, and levels of cortisol in saliva between occasions and among conditioned and control subjects, respectively. Since we expected to find elevated NKCA only in experimental subjects (group 1), single-tailed Student's *t*-tests were computed to prove our hypothesis.

Protocol Utrecht: Experimental design I

Six male subjects (mean age 25.7 years) participated in this study. They were randomly assigned to the control (*N* = 3) or experimental (*N* = 3) group. They were treated for three consecutive days, with the test trial being on day 4. Before participation in the experiment subjects were told that the aim of the experiment was to determine the effects of epinephrine on four consecutive days. Epinephrine or saline (as a control) would be administered by means of an injection or a bitter tasting drink. They were told that after the administration some people would experience side-effects which would be comparable to sensations after mild physical activity. It was made clear to them there were several experimental groups, which received epinephrine or saline on differing days. No further information was provided, i.e. subjects did not know that they were participating in a learning experiment.

Immediately after arrival at the laboratory at 8.30 a.m., an intravenous catheter was inserted into the anticubital vein. The cannula was kept open by an obturator which was removed for blood drawing. The first blood sample was taken after a rest of half an hour. Subsequently, a bitter tasting drink was offered (CS) followed by an injection with the UCS.

Immunologic analyses. Heparin blood was diluted 1:1 with MEM-Tris. Peripheral blood mononuclear cells were isolated by Ficoll-Paque density centrifugation (20 min, 400 *g*). The interphase was removed and cells were washed with MEM-Tris (10 min, 100 *g*). To remove monocytes, cells were resuspended in MEM-Tris with 20 per cent FCS at a concentration of 10×10^6/ml. Carbonyl-iron was added and under regular shaking, cells were incubated for 30–45 min at 37 degrees centigrade. Carbonyl-iron and monocytes were removed with a magnet and remaining cells were washed with MEM-Tris and resuspended in RPMI-5 per cent FCS. Activity of NK cells was tested according to the protocol used by the Trier group. Results are given for the 50:1 co-cultures. NK cells were phenotyped by use of CD16 monoclonals (Becton-Dickinson) and were analysed by FACSSCAN analysis according to standard procedures.

Data analysis. Changes in NKCA and number of NK cells relative to baseline measures were calculated. To test the differences in changes between control and experimental groups Student's two-tailed *t* tests for independent measures were used.

Protocol Utrecht: Experimental design II

Seven male subjects (mean age 24.4 years) participated in the second Utrecht conditioning experiments. During experiment II no control subjects were investigated, for it was assumed that a control group would only make sense if a conditioned immune reaction could be induced in the experimental group. In this experiment the same CS (sherbet sweet) was used as in the Trier study. Acquisition trials were executed on four days, while on the fifth day the test trial was performed. For the other procedures, the same protocol was maintained and the same information given to the subjects as in Expt I. They were told the sherbet sweet was administered to distract them from the experimental conditions.

Immunologic analyses. To assess the influence of monocytes on the NKCA, the assay was performed under the same procedure, but without removing the monocytes. To test the sensitivity of NK cells for epinephrine, cells of the first blood sample (before epinephrine was administered) of day 1 and day 5 were stimulated *in vitro* with epinephrine. Mononuclear cells were incubated for 7 min at 37 degrees centigrade with epinephrine in the concentrations of 10^{-4} and 10^{-8} M. After extensive washing with MEM-Tris, the NKCA was determined as usual.

Data analysis. Differences from baseline levels were tested with two-tailed Student's *t*-tests for paired data.

Results

Trier study

Figure 1 summarizes the changes in natural killer cell activity relative to individual baseline values in experimental and control subjects. On day 1 epinephrine administration caused a significant increase in NKCA at 20 minutes post-injection in the experimental group compared to saline injected control subjects. This effect was observed at all three effector-target cell ratios (100:1, 50:1 and 25:1), with the most pronounced difference in the 50:1 co-cultures ($t(12) = 3.16$, $p < .01$). The reaction was accompanied by a rise in the proportion of NK cells relative to total peripheral lymphocytes at 20 min post-injection ($p < .05$; Fig. 2) which might have contributed to the increase in NKCA.

On the conditioning test trial, day 5, experimental subjects again showed a significant elevation of NKCA, although they were injected with saline on this day. This response was significantly higher compared to control subjects who received the same treatment as on day 1 ($t(12) = 2.77$, $p < .01$; Fig. 1). Remarkably, on day 5 no change in the total number of peripheral CD57+ cells was observed in the experimental group (Fig. 2). Following the subcutaneous injection of 0.2 mg epinephrine on day 1, plasma epinephrine concentrations were significantly elevated at 20 min post-injection ($t = 2.75$; $p < .05$). No respective alteration was found after

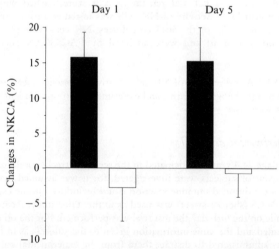

Figure 1. Trier study: Mean absolute changes ($\pm$SEM) from baseline of natural killer cell activity (NKCA) in experimental ($N = 7$) and control ($N = 7$) groups in the 50:1 co-cultures 20 min after epinephrine injection. ■, experimental group; □, control group.

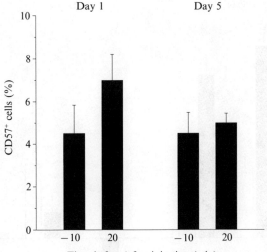

Figure 2. Trier study: Mean absolute percentage of CD57+ cells (±(SEM) in the peripheral blood of experimental (*N* = 7) and control (*N* = 7) groups 20 minutes after epinephrine injection.

saline administration on the conditioning test trial (day 5). Moreover, neither on day 1 nor on day 5 did salivary cortisol differ between experimental and control groups at any time point (all *p* > .1). On both days cortisol concentrations showed a steady decline from the first to the last sample reflecting circadian rhythm fluctuations during morning hours. Thus, no stress-related increase in cortisol levels could be observed.

Utrecht: Experiment I

Figures 3 and 4 summarize the results of the experimental and control groups for the NKCA and the percentage of NK cells (CD16+). On day 1, significant changes in NKCA compared with the control group were found after 5 and 45 min (*t*(4) = 5.3, *p* < .01 and *t*(4) = 5.2, *p* < .05 respectively). Comparable results were found for the changes in number of CD16+ cells on day 1 (*t*(4) = 3.7, *p* < .05 and *t*(4) = 3.2, *p* < .05, respectively). On day 4 no significant differences in NKCA change were found for the two groups on the two time points, although there was a trend for an increase in NKCA for the control group. However, it was found that the number of CD16+ NK cells rose significantly for the control group compared with the experimental group (*t*(4) = −4.7, *p* < .05 and *t*(4) = −3.0, *p* = .05). It was concluded that no conditioned NKCA was induced.

Utrecht: Experiment II

Figures 5 and 6 summarize the results of the second conditioning experiments performed in Utrecht. Again no conditioned immune response could be induced. On day 1 the NKCA increased significantly (*t*(6) = −6.3, *p* < .01 and *t*(6) = −6.2,

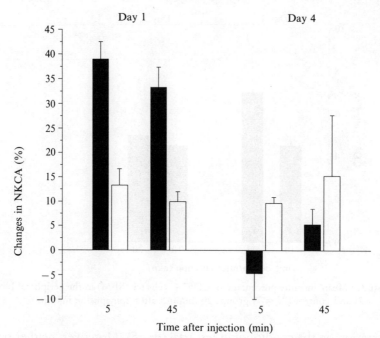

Figure 3. Utrecht study I: Mean absolute changes (±SEM) from baseline of natural killer cell activity (NKCA) in experimental ($N = 3$) and control ($N = 3$) groups in the 50:1 co-cultures 5 and 45 min after epinephrine injection. ■, experimental group; □, control group.

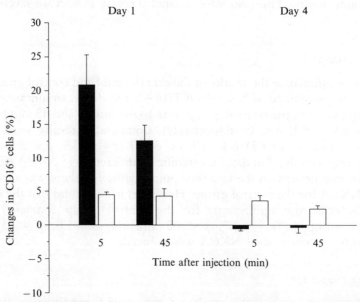

Figure 4. Utrecht study I: Mean absolute changes (±SEM) from baseline of percentage CD16+ cells in the peripheral blood of experimental ($N = 3$) and control ($N = 3$) groups 5 and 45 min after epinephrine injection. ■, experimental group; □, control group.

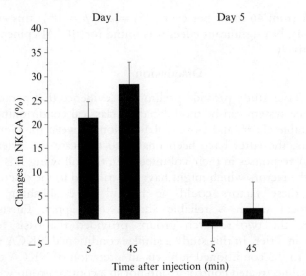

Figure 5. Utrecht study II: Mean absolute changes ($\pm$ SEM) from baseline of natural killer cell activity (NKCA) in experimental group ($N = 7$) in the 50:1 co-cultures 5 and 45 min after epinephrine injection.

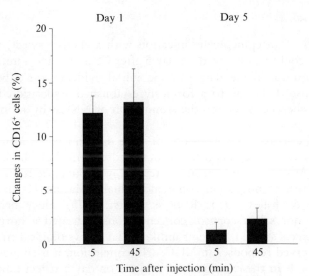

Figure 6. Utrecht study II: Mean absolute changes ($\pm$ SEM) from baseline of percentage CD16+ cells in the peripheral blood of experimental group ($N = 7$) 5 and 45 min after epinephrine injection.

$p < .01$, respectively), but not on day 5 ($t < 1$). To assess the effects of the monocytes on NKCA, the assay was also performed without removing the monocytes. On day 1 the NKCA was increased ($t(3) = -4.6$, $p < .05$ and $t(3) = -5.5$, $p < .05$, respectively), but again no conditioned effect on day 5 was found ($t < 1$).

Sensitivity of NK cells for stimulation by epinephrine was altered when compared with the basal levels. On day 1 stimulation with 10^{-4} M epinephrine resulted in a decrease in NKCA from 46 to 37 per cent ($t(5) = 2.6$, $p = .05$); this effect was not seen on day 5 ($t < 1$). No significant effect was found for 10^{-8} M epinephrine on day 1 or day 5, respectively.

Discussion

The results of the Trier study provide preliminary evidence that parameters of the human body defence system can be modulated by classical conditioning. However, in spite of considerable efforts and close collaboration between the German and the Dutch investigators, the latter have been unable to replicate the Trier findings of conditioned NKCA responses in their volunteers. In the following it is attempted to elucidate some of the factors which might have contributed to the discrepant results. Consideration of these factors could be helpful in establishing an immune conditioning protocol which is reliable and easy to apply. Furthermore, the discussion between the two research groups provided the basis for a second conditioning study in Trier. In this study a similar conditioned NKCA response was found. In contrast to the conditioned subjects an alteration of NKCA could neither be monitored in a saline-treated control group nor in a control group which received the stimuli in a non-paired manner (Buske-Kirschbaum, Kirschbaum, Stierle, Lehnert & Hellhammer, 1992).

Discussion on Trier results

After four pairings of an epinephrine injection with a sherbet sweet, a significant increase in NKCA could be observed on day 5 after CS and saline administration in the experimental group. These data provide initial evidence for a behaviourally conditioned response (CR) due to a formerly established association between the previously neutral sherbet sweet and the stimulation of NKCA by an injection with epinephrine.

There may be alternative interpretations of these data, however. Most important, a stress-induced secretion of epinephrine from the adrenal medulla might have led to increased NKCA. As one example of such stressors, venepuncture is known to affect epinephrine and cortisol output in some individuals (Mason, Hartley, Kotchen, Mougey, Ricketts & Jones, 1973; Rose & Hurst, 1975). Since neither plasma epinephrine levels nor saliva cortisol concentrations indicated a hormonal stress response in the subjects studied, it seems unlikely that a physiological stress response modulated the observed responses in NKCA. In conclusion, it is suggested that the elevated NKCA levels in the experimental subjects on day 5 reflect a behaviourally conditioned response.

Discussion on Utrecht results

In Expt I no conditioned effect of the NKCA was found in the experimental group on day 4. It was found that the NKCA and the number of CD16 + cells of the control group showed a tendency towards even higher increases than the experimental group. It was hypothesized that the lymphocytes of the experimental group had become less responsive to endogenously released epinephrine due to a high dose of agonist on the three preceding days. It is well known that chronic high doses of agonist may affect receptor affinity or even receptor number (Mills & Dimsdale, 1988). To test this phenomenon, in Expt II mononuclear cells were incubated with two different concentrations of agonist before the NKCA was performed. A slight difference in sensitivity to 10^{-4} M epinephrine was found. This suggests that a high agonist concentration on some consecutive days has a significant effect on epinephrine receptor status in the experimental group so that sensitivity for the agonist is decreased on day 5. Since in their first experiment the Utrecht group removed monocytes before performing the NK cell assay (in contrast to the Trier group) it was thought that monocytes might have mediated the conditioned NKCA response. Results from Kavelaars, Ballieux & Heijnen (1989) showed that peripheral blood B cells in the presence of monocytes are capable of producing β-endorphin (βE) in response to stimulation with corticotropin-releasing factor (CRF) and arginine-vasopressin (AVP). It is well known that βE influence the NKCA (Kay, Allen & Morley 1984; Mathews, Fröhlich, Sibbit & Bankhurst, 1983). It was thought that epinephrine would trigger this mechanism. However, performing the NKCA assay in the presence of monocytes did not result in a conditioned increase in activity. This indicates that they probably do not play an intermediary role in the conditioned effect on the NKCA as found by the Trier group.

Conclusion

Although after their first experiments the Utrecht group tried to parallel the experimental settings of the Trier group, it is possible that small differences in protocol for which it was hard to control still existed. What are the reasons for the discrepant results obtained in the two research groups? At least two suggestions can be made.

First of all, one important difference in the two protocols was the information given to the subjects before the start of the experiment. In contrast to the Trier group the Dutch researchers were obliged by the local medical ethical committee to inform the subjects of the substance they were injected with and its possible physical side-effects. Although they were not told that they were participating in a conditioning experiment, it is possible that this knowledge influenced the conditioning results because expectations on the experiment were set. Several researchers studied the influence of expectation on placebo responses. Schachter & Singer (1962) showed the importance of information for the (physical) interpretation of emotion-arousing situations. Subjects injected with epinephrine and informed about its true side-effects did not change their mood to correspond to the situation in which they found themselves in contrast with the mis- and uninformed groups. In other words, the same situation produced different effects and emotions in people whose emotional tone had been altered physiologically. Penick & Fisher (1965) injected subjects with epinephrine and varied the information given. Subjects who received the suggestion of epinephrine-like effects had higher free fatty acid and glucose concentrations in peripheral blood and a greater heart rate response compared with the subjects who received a sedative expectation. The relation between expectancy and placebo effects is extensively described in a meta-analysis by Ross & Olson (1981). Some of the conclusions they made were that in pharmacological placebo studies: 1. the direction of the placebo effect seems to be related to the drug under study; 2. the strength of the placebo effect is proportional to the strength of the drug effect; and 3. the 'side-effects' of placebos are often similar to the side-effects of the drugs to which they are being compared. Although some studies report no effects, standard placebo effects are more common. Because of these findings, the authors state that placebos presumably can have an impact only if subjects hold expectancies about the placebo's effects. Although these studies cannot explain the discrepancies in conditioning results observed, they show the importance of expectancies. According to the studies cited, the difference in protocol would even favour the Utrecht group because their subjects expected epinephrine-like effects which should facilitate a standard placebo effect in the expected direction.

A second suggestion as to why the Trier results could not be replicated by the Utrecht group may be that cultural differences might have affected the outcome of the conditioning experiment. For example, the Dutch investigators would have had difficulties in recruiting subjects without giving them extensive information about the experiment even if the medical ethical committee would have permitted this. Dutch subjects in general tend to be very critical of experiments in which they participate. The Trier group did not encounter these problems. It was relatively easy to recruit enough subjects who were not informed about the substance with which they were injected. This is an intriguing difference in compliance (to authority?) which we hypothesized could be ascribed to cultural factors. Indeed Payer (1988) mentioned a cultural bias in medical science and differences in patient attitude in health care practice. Although the authors could not find any reports on the effects of cultural dissimilarities on learning processes in the literature, this difference may well have influenced the results. One example of the importance of attitudinal differences was described by Jensen & Karoly (1991) who showed that manipulation of motivation resulted in larger placebo effects for highly motivated subjects.

A minor difference between the Trier and the Utrecht protocol was the timing of blood taking. While in the Trier experiment blood samples were obtained at 20 min after epinephrine/saline injection, the Utrecht group took blood at 5 and 45 min post-injection. However, in previous experiments the Utrecht group did not observe significant differences in NKCA when samples were obtained either 20 or 45 min after epinephrine administration (unpublished data). Thus it is most likely that the different timing in taking blood does not help to interpret the different results obtained in the two laboratories.

In conclusion, it appears difficult to discover the reasons for the conflicting results reported here. From the present data it could be speculated that in an experimental setting Pavlovian conditioning of the immune response does not yield robust effects. In contrast to most studies in animals, a given conditioning protocol might work in one location but fail to elicit conditioned responses in a different setting. It is quite possible that the mild nature of the CS used in laboratory experiments contributes to this failure. Ethical restraints do not permit the exact reproduction of situations encountered in a clinical setting, which have been reported to induce successfully anticipatory immune suppression (Bovbjerg et al., 1990).

Nevertheless, both groups stress the importance of this line of research. First, it will be important to find out which elements in the experimental set-up contribute significantly to the conditioned response. Besides its heuristic value, it may help to elucidate whether learning processes are linked to the onset and course of disease in man. A possible application of these basic findings could be a combination of pharmacological and behavioural therapeutic strategies. It is reasonable to assume that an association of drug application (US) with a formerly neutral stimulus (CS) in a clinical setting could result in a modification of immune parameters after exposure to the CS alone. In this case, patients may benefit from the combined treatment because the desired therapeutic effects could then be gained with a reduction of side-effects induced by medication.

References

Ader, R. & Cohen, N. (1982). Behaviorally conditioned immunosuppression and murine systemic lupus erythematosus. *Science*, **215**, 1534–1536.

Ader, R. & Cohen, N. (1985). CNS-immune system interactions: Conditioning phenomena. *Behavioral and Brain Sciences*, **8**, 379–394.

Ader, R. & Cohen, N. (1991). The influence of conditioning on immune responses. In R. Ader, D. L. Felten & N. Cohen (Eds), *Psychoneuroimmunology*, pp. 611–646. San Diego, CA: Academic Press.

Bauch, H.-J., Kelsch, U. & Hauss, W. H. (1986). Einfache, schnelle, selektive und quantitative Bestimmung von Adrenalin und Noradrenalin im Plasma durch Kombination von Flüssigextraktion, HPLC-Trennung und elektrochemischer Detektion. *Journal of Clinical Chemistry and Clinical Biochemistry*, **24**, 651–658.

Berkenbosch, F., van Oers, J., del Rey, A., Tilders, F. & Besedovsky, H. (1987). Corticotropin-releasing factor-producing neurons in the rat activated by interleukin-1. *Science*, **238**, 524–526.

Blalock, J. E. (1984). The immune system as a sensory organ. *Journal of Immunology*, **132**, 1067–1070.

Bost, K. L. (1988). Hormone and neuropeptide receptors on mononuclear leukocytes. *Progress in Allergy*, **43**, 68–83.

Bovbjerg, D. H., Redd, W. H., Maier, L. A., Holland, J. C., Lesko, L. M., Niedzwiecki, D., Rubni, S. C. & Hakes, T. B. (1990). Anticipatory immune suppression and nausea in women receiving cyclic chemotherapy for ovarian cancer. *Journal of Consulting and Clinical Psychology*, **58**, 153–157.

Buske-Kirschbaum, A., Kirschbaum, C., Stierle, H. E., Lehnert, H. & Hellhammer, D. H. (1992). Classical conditioning of natural killer cell activity (NKCA) in humans. *Psychosomatic Medicine*, **54**, 123–132.

Crary, B., Hauser, S. L., Borysenko, M., Kutz, I., Hoban, C., Ault, K. A., Weiner, H. L. & Benson, H. (1983). Epinephrine-induced changes in the distribution of lymphocyte subsets in peripheral blood of humans. *Journal of Immunology*, **131**, 1178–1181.

Felten, S. Y. & Felten, D. L. (1991). Innervation of lymphoid tissue. In R. Ader, D. L. Felten & N. Cohen (Eds), *Psychoneuroimmunology*, pp. 27–69. San Diego, CA: Academic Press.

Ghanta, V. K., Hiramoto, R. N., Solvason, B. & Spector, N. H. (1985). Neural and environmental influences on neoplasia and conditioning of NK activity. *Journal of Immunology*, **135**, 848–852.

Hellhammer, D. H., Kirschbaum, C. & Belkien, L. (1987). Measurement of salivary cortisol under psychological stimulation. In J. N. Hingtgen, D. Hellhammer & G. Huppmann (Eds), *Advanced Methods in Psychobiology*, pp. 281–289. Toronto: Hogrefe.

Herberman, R. & Ortaldo, J. (1981). Natural killer cells: Their role in defenses against disease. *Science*, **214**, 24–29.

Jensen, M. P. & Karoly, P. (1991). Motivation and expectancy factors in symptom perception: A laboratory study of the placebo effect. *Psychosomatic Medicine*, **53**, 144–152.

Kavelaars, A., Ballieux, R. E. & Heijnen, C. J. (1989). The role of IL-1 in the corticotropin-releasing factor and arginine-vasopressin-induced secretion of immunoreactive beta-endorphine by human blood mononuclear cells. *Journal of Immunology*, **142**, 2338–2343.

Kay, N., Allen, J. & Morley, J. E. (1984). Endorphins stimulate normal human peripheral blood lymphocyte natural killer cell activity. *Life Sciences*, **35**, 53–59.

Kirschbaum, C., Strasburger, C. J., Jammers, W. & Hellhammer, D. H. (1989). Cortisol and behavior: 1. Adaptation of a radioimmunoassay kit for reliable and inexpensive salivary cortisol determination. *Pharmacology Biochemistry and Behavior*, **34**, 747–751.

Mason, J. W., Hartley, H., Kotchen, T. A., Mougey, E. H., Ricketts, P. T. & Jones, L. R. G. (1973). Plasma cortisol and norepinephrine responses in anticipation of muscular exercise. *Psychosomatic Medicine*, **35**, 406–414.

Mathews, P. M., Fröhlich, C. J., Sibbit, W. L. & Bankhurst, A. D. (1983). Enhancement of natural cytotoxicity by β-endorphin. *Journal of Immunology*, **130**, 1658–1662.

Mills, P. J. & Dimsdale, J. E. (1988). The promise of receptor studies in psychophysiologic research. *Psychosomatic Medicine*, **50**, 555–566.

Payer, L. (1988). *Medicine and Culture: Varieties of Treatment in the United States, England, West Germany, and France*. New York: Henry Holt.

Penick, S. B. & Fisher, S. (1965). Drug-set interaction: Psychological and physiological effects of epinephrine under differential expectations. *Psychosomatic Medicine*, **27**, 177–182.

Rose, M. R. & Hurst, M. W. (1975). Plasma cortisol and growth hormone responses to intravenous catheterization. *Journal of Human Stress*, **1**, 22–36.

Ross, M. & Olson, J. M. (1981). An expectancy-attribution model of the effects of placebos. *Psychological Review*, **88**, 408–437.

Sapolsky, R., Rivier, C., Yamamoto, G., Plotsky, P. & Vale, W. (1987). Interleukin-1 stimulates the secretion of hypothalamic corticotropin-releasing factor. *Science*, **238**, 522–524.

Schachter, S. & Singer, J. (1962). Cognitive, social and physiological determinants of emotional state. *Psychological Review*, **69**, 379–399.

Tönnesen, E., Tönnesen, J. & Christensen, N. (1984). Augmentation of cytotoxicity by natural killer cells (NK) after adrenaline administration in man. *Acta Pathologica Microbiologica Immunologica Scandinavica*, **C.92**, 81–83.

British Journal of Clinical Psychology (1992), **31**, 473–483   *Printed in Great Britain*

Psychosocial aspects of cardiac rehabilitation in Europe

Stan Maes*

Health Psychology, Leiden University, PO Box 9555, Wassenaarseweg 52, 2300 RB Leiden, The Netherlands

While the present objectives of cardiac rehabilitation include recovery or restoration of everyday behaviour and secondary prevention, the effects of the traditional exercise-based cardiac rehabilitation programmes are quite modest.

It is argued that psychological interventions may affect these targets more easily, since there is evidence from controlled studies that psychological interventions may have beneficial effects on psychosocial recovery, compliance with medical advice and cardiovascular morbidity and mortality. As a consequence one may expect that psychologists would be at least part-time members of most cardiac rehabilitation teams in European countries.

In order to get an impression of the position of psychologists and the share of psychosocial care in cardiac rehabilitation in Europe, a questionnaire was sent out to two or three individuals in each European country. Health care professionals from 16 European countries returned their completed questionnaires on time.

Among other things, the results show that in general social workers and psychologists, who may be considered the main potential agents for psychosocial care, are largely underrepresented in cardiac rehabilitation teams.

As far as psychologists are concerned, the number involved in cardiac rehabilitation varies significantly from country to country. Three groups of countries could be distinguished: a group consisting of The Netherlands, Austria, and Italy, where psychologists are fairly well represented; a second one consisting of Norway, Finland and Belgium, where small numbers of psychologists are involved in cardiac rehabilitation; and a third group (the largest) consisting of Switzerland, Poland, Czechoslovakia, Denmark, Ireland, Sweden, the UK, Greece, Portugal and Turkey, where the number of psychologists is negligible.

Ischaemic heart disease in Europe

As most patients who qualify for cardiac rehabilitation suffer from ischaemic heart diseases, it is important to realize that these diseases are the main cause of death in developed countries. Of the 11 million deaths that occur annually in these countries, about 2.4 million or 22 per cent are due to ischaemic heart disease (World Health Organization, 1989). At the same time, however, there are huge differences in mortality due to these diseases between the various European countries. In fact, mortality rates for ischaemic heart diseases are about three times higher in several former Eastern Bloc and northern European countries (including Czechoslovakia, Bulgaria, Hungary, Ireland, the United Kingdom, Finland, Sweden, Denmark, Iceland and Norway) than in most Mediterranean countries (including Italy,

* Requests for reprints.

Yugoslavia, Greece, Portugal, Spain and France), with other European countries forming a middle group. Although morbidity data would provide a more detailed picture, they are scarce or patchy and are not collected in a uniform manner. For example 'myocardial insufficiency' is the leading diagnosis in Germany, but has no obvious equivalent in other countries (O'Brien, 1984). The only source which can provide us with comparable morbidity data for Europe is the World Health Organization Monica (multinational MONItoring of trends and determinants in Cardiovascular disease) project, but until now only data on mortality and risk factor status have been published (World Health Organization, 1989).

Objectives of cardiac rehabilitation

A meeting in Noordwijk aan Zee (The Netherlands), organized by the Regional Office for Europe of the WHO in 1967, reflected current opinion 25 years ago that physical training should be the cornerstone of cardiac rehabilitation designed to improve physical fitness and return the patient to work. Over the last decade the objectives of cardiac rehabilitation have become both more comprehensive and more realistic. Indeed, there is wide agreement now that cardiac rehabilitation should facilitate the patient's return to his or her usual way of life before the incident not only in a professional sense, but also in a much wider physical, personal and social sense (Mulcahy, 1990). This implies that restoring everyday behaviour (e.g. visiting friends, driving a car, preparing meals, working in the garden, bicycling, doing some repair jobs in and around the house or making love) is now much more the ultimate goal of cardiac rehabilitation. In other words, the quality of (everyday) life has become equally as important as social reintegration in a professional or vocational sense.

But although the restoration of the patient's way of life before the incident is the final goal of cardiac rehabilitation, two reservations have to be made. Firstly, it is obvious that the degree to which this end-point can be reached is largely dependent on physical limitations, which are related to the severity of the incident. Secondly, there is a growing awareness that secondary prevention should be added to the traditional goals of cardiac rehabilitation. Secondary prevention implies a reduction of cardiovascular mortality and morbidity, including further incidents and complications, through pharmacological therapy, surgery and risk factor modification. This implies that the patient must be encouraged to return to his or her former way of life, with the exception of life-style aspects related to hyperlipidaemia, tobacco smoking, hypertension, diabetes, excessive weight, lack of physical exercise, alcohol abuse and excessive forms of stress.

Based on these insights, cardiac rehabilitation can be defined as the coordinated efforts of various health professionals and non-professionals to help the patient return to his or her former way of life, taking into account possible limitations brought about by the incident and secondary prevention measures for gaining control over the progression of the disease.

The current cardiac rehabilitation programme in Europe

A programme of rehabilitation generally starts after the first or acute-care phase, when patients are transferred from the coronary care or intensive care unit to a hospital ward. During this second stage, apart from pharmacological treatment, rehabilitation consists mainly of the provision of information to patients about their physical condition and the consequences of this for treatment and daily life, including life-style changes. In addition, the average patient receives a form of physical therapy in order to restore his or her physical condition. After about two weeks the patient is dismissed from the hospital and can then enrol in an exercise-based out-patient rehabilitation programme at the hospital. In most European countries, patients who take part in such a programme travel on average three times a week to and from the hospital in order to attend physical exercise sessions for a period of eight to 16 weeks. At the end of this third phase the average patient is considered to be rehabilitated, implying that he or she should be able to resume normal daily activities (for example, work, leisure activities and role in the family) as much as possible and should have integrated life-style changes into his or her way of life that could prevent a future incident of cardiac arrest. In Germany, however, the standard form of cardiac rehabilitation during this phase is different: cardiac rehabilitation patients are treated in rehabilitation clinics for six to eight weeks after dismissal from the general hospital. In these clinics, apart from medical examinations and pharmacological treatment, patients are offered physical training programmes designed to promote physical recovery, as well as psychological forms of care including stress management and interventions aimed at stimulating life-style changes and social reintegration (Klapp & Dahme, 1988; Langosch, 1985). In Italy, there seems to exist a mixture of forms of clinical and out of clinic rehabilitation during this phase. In several countries, groups organized by cardiac patients offer cardiac rehabilitation patients, during a fourth phase, the opportunity to join sports or exercise groups under the direct or indirect supervision of a health professional in their home town or area. This fourth phase can last several years and is usually called the resocialization phase. For the small group of patients who do not recover as expected, in most countries there are a few rehabilitation clinics or departments where clinical rehabilitation is offered.

It should be noted, however, that there are important differences between and within European countries. At one extreme there are countries or health care centres within a country where forms of professional care other than pharmacological treatment, surgery and medical advice after dismissal from the hospital are considered too expensive or unnecessary. At the other extreme there are countries and centres which offer a wide range of interventions, including psychosocial interventions, in addition to standard medical care and exercise training, sometimes even in a clinical setting, as in Germany.

Effectiveness of exercise-based cardiac rehabilitation

The effectiveness of exercise-based rehabilitation programmes (consisting of pharmacological therapy, medical advice and on average three sessions a week of physical exercise training for a period of two to three months) has been seriously questioned over the last few years. This is mainly because exercise training does not seem to have a substantial influence on traditional cardiac rehabilitation targets such as survival, return to work and physical fitness.

Firstly, with the exception of a study by Kallio, Hämäläinen, Hakkila & Luurile (1979), individual controlled trials of exercise-based rehabilitation programmes for myocardial infarction patients have failed to demonstrate significant effects on cardiac morbidity and mortality (Lipkin, 1991). In contrast to this, Oldrige, Guyatt, Fischer & Rimm (1988) showed favourable effects of exercise training on mortality in a recent review in which they calculated by means of meta-analysis a combined effect for 22 randomized exercise trials carried out during the last two decades. Results of meta-analyses deserve cautious interpretation, however, since there is a trend in the literature not to publish studies with negative results and since pooling of data from very different patient populations and different exercise programmes may create important artifacts. In other words, as far as effects on morbidity and mortality are concerned, if there is not a lack of evidence, there is at least a lack of randomized trials with populations large enough to demonstrate effects.

Secondly, most randomized exercise trials fail to show any effects on return to work (Bär & Vonken, 1990; Diederiks, 1982). This should not surprise us, since attending physical exercise sessions three times a week for three months in a (sometimes distant) hospital may keep people longer in a patient role and make it actually physically impossible to be at their workplace at the same time.

Lastly, although physical exercise has been shown to increase patients' maximal exercise capacity by about 20 per cent in comparison to controls at the end of an exercise programme, this benefit seems to be completely lost one year later (Bär & Vonken, 1990). However, Bär & Vonken showed in a recent randomized exercise trial that some subgroups may benefit more than others from this treatment.

As the high expectations of exercise-based rehabilitation programmes with respect to physical recovery gradually dropped to more modest levels, promoters of exercise training have claimed that it has important effects on psychosocial recovery and the quality of daily life, targets which have become of increasing importance. Randomized studies show that exercise programmes have some effect on psychosocial variables such as anxiety and depression by the end of the programmes. These changes appear to parallel the physical effects, but seem to disappear within a few months (Erdman, Duivenvoorden, Verhage, Kazemier & Hugenholtz, 1984). As far as modification of risk factors through pharmacological therapy and life-style changes is concerned, the effect of the average exercise-based rehabilitation programme is even more questionable. On average about half of coronary heart disease patients do not seem to comply with medical advice concerning smoking, medication, physical activity, diet or weight reduction one year after the incident (Bär et al., 1990; Burling, Singleton, Bigelow, Baile & Gottlieb, 1984; Dishman, Sallis & Orenstein, 1985). While these rates in themselves are a cause for concern, it is obvious that non-compliance will only increase further with time (Heller, Frank, Kornfeld, Wilson & Malm, 1982).

The consequence of these research results is that exercise-based rehabilitation programmes after hospital discharge have been seriously questioned. While some are of the opinion that these forms of cardiac rehabilitation may not be necessary, others think that the modest effects of the present programmes are mainly due to the fact that standard programmes are offered to all patients, while some subgroups would profit more than others from these programmes (Lipkin, 1991). In addition, there is a growing consensus that psychosocial interventions are probably more effective for psychosocial recovery and increasing compliance with medical advice (Bär *et al.*, 1990).

Psychosocial interventions in cardiac rehabilitation

As already stated, psychosocial interventions may affect rehabilitation outcomes in two ways. Firstly, they may facilitate psychosocial recovery, including the return to everyday activities. Secondly, they may play an important role in secondary prevention, by improving compliance with medical advice concerning medication and life-style changes. There are two principal strategies available for both of these avenues.

The first is to improve the communication and psychological intervention skills of existing health care professionals, most of whom fail to realize that influencing behaviour implies skills which go beyond the provision of information. In order to be effective, a communication or message must at least: (a) get the individual's attention (many messages do not even reach the patient, e.g. because of lack of time or lack of an organized form of care); (b) be understood (many communications are not fully understood by the patient); (c) be retained (much of the information provided is forgotten even within minutes after being given); (d) be accepted (even if understood and retained, the advice may be in conflict with the patient's goals or beliefs); (e) lead to behavioural change (not every patient who is convinced of the relevance of specific advice is able to follow that advice, e.g. many patients want to stop smoking but are not able to do so); and (f) lead to maintenance of the new behaviour (many patients stop following the advice after some time for various reasons) (Leventhal, Prohaska & Hirschman, 1985).

The second avenue is to add psychosocial professionals to rehabilitation teams. This is a trend which is very visible in some countries (e.g. The Netherlands), but not in others (e.g. the UK). In The Netherlands the number of nurses involved in cardiac rehabilitation after dismissal from the hospital decreased by about 50 per cent over the last 10 years, while the number of social workers and especially psychologists increased considerably over the same period (Soons & Bär, 1990). This is in sharp contrast to the situation in the UK, where cardiac rehabilitation seems to be the almost exclusive territory of medical doctors and paramedical personnel (Davidson, Green & Stansfield, 1988). It is obvious that psychosocial professionals can be involved in different ways. Whereas in The Netherlands some 10 years ago cardiac patients were referred to social workers and psychologists primarily on an individual basis for the treatment of severe psychosocial problems, the current trend is for these professionals gradually to offer more systematic forms of group interventions to large numbers of patients in close cooperation with other team members (Maes, van Foreest, Smulders, van Elderen & Bruggemans, 1986).

The increase in systematic psychosocial interventions has made it possible to evaluate their effectiveness. Apart from unstructured forms of interventions, at least two types of structured interventions can be distinguished in daily practice and in the research literature. On the one hand, there are controlled studies of stress management interventions which aim at influencing morbidity and mortality via psychosocial changes. On the other hand, we find controlled studies of behaviour modification and health education interventions, which are directed at the same goals via the improvement of compliance with medical advice. Many psychosocial programmes consist, however, of a combination of stress management and health education. At present, there are more than 20 randomized studies of various psychosocial interventions in cardiac rehabilitation. While not all of these studies produced consistent results, a critical review shows that they can have beneficial effects on reported stress levels, professional reintegration, necessary life-style changes (with respect to diet and nutrition, physical activity and smoking), risk factors and even morbidity and mortality (Bundy, 1989, van Dixhoorn, 1991; van Elderen, 1991; Maes, van Elderen & Bruggemans, 1987).

However, there is a very wide gap between the results of these studies, or even the kind of psychosocial interventions under study, and the daily practice of psychosocial interventions in cardiac rehabilitation. This will be illustrated with the results of a survey, which are described below.

Method

Psychosocial interventions in Europe: A survey

Design. In order to get an impression of what is going on in Europe in terms of psychosocial interventions in cardiac rehabilitation, a questionnaire was sent to two or three individuals in each European country who were directly or indirectly involved in cardiac rehabilitation. Twenty-seven questionnaires from 16 European countries – Austria (A), Belgium (B), Czechoslovakia (Cz), Denmark (Dk), Finland (F), Greece (G), Ireland (Ir), Italy (I), The Netherlands (NL), Norway (N), Poland (P), Portugal (Pr), Switzerland (CH), Sweden (Sw), Turkey (T) and the UK (UK) – were returned on time. About half of the respondents consisted of medical doctors, the other half of psychologists. When the answers of two independent respondents within a country were not in line with each other, the 'average answer' was considered closest to the reality in that country. Although a higher number of respondents would have undoubtedly enhanced the reliability of the results, I believe that the general trends, which are described below, offer a fairly realistic picture of what is going on in Europe today.

Results

Characteristics of cardiac rehabilitation in different countries

According to our respondents, the percentage of cardiac patients taking part in an exercise-based rehabilitation programme after dismissal from hospital varies considerably from country to country. While there is apparently no such form of rehabilitation in Portugal or Turkey, exercise-based forms of cardiac rehabilitation seem to be offered to less than 20 per cent of patients in Ireland (where these programmes are virtually non-existent), Finland, Greece, Czechoslovakia and Poland, to between 20 and 40 per cent of patients in Norway, Denmark, Switzerland and Belgium, and to between 40 and 60 per cent of patients in The Netherlands, the UK, Italy, Sweden, Germany and Austria. In general one could say that these data show a trend in which cardiac rehabilitation is more established in the richer (mostly north- and central-western) than in the poorer (mostly southern and eastern) European countries. Finland being the exception, this trend is confirmed by the fact that Ireland and Italy do not follow the predominant trend within their region;

Ireland is a relatively poor country with a low national health budget in comparison with other Western European countries whereas Italy is a country with a much higher national income than the other southern European countries and even has the highest number of physicians per 10 000 inhabitants in Europe, e.g. about three times higher than in Portugal or Spain (Organization for Economic Cooperation & Development, 1990).

In countries where there is (at least for a minority of patients) a systematic form of cardiac rehabilitation after dismissal from hospital, we asked respondents how frequently various professionals were part of the rehabilitation team. The general trends in the answers indicate that medical doctors are regular team members in virtually all countries. Physiotherapists or sports trainers are also regular members of the rehabilitation team in many countries, with the exception of Austria, Denmark and Poland, where they are present in less than half of the settings. For nurses, there are important differences between countries: they seem to be part of the rehabilitation team in less than 20 per cent of the settings in Switzerland, Sweden, Belgium and Italy; between 20 and 50 per cent of the settings in Denmark, The Netherlands and Poland; and in nearly all settings in Austria, Czechoslovakia, Finland and the UK. For dieticians, there is also an important variance: they appear to be team members in less than 20 per cent of the cases in Poland, Switzerland, Sweden and Belgium; 20 to 50 per cent of the cases in Italy and Denmark; and in over 75 per cent of the cases in all other countries. Social workers are said not to be staff members in Switzerland, Italy, Poland and the UK; to be staff members in fewer than 30 per cent of the settings in Austria, Czechoslovakia, Denmark, Finland, Sweden and Belgium; and in as many as 80 per cent of the settings in The Netherlands. Psychologists seem to be staff members in virtually every country, but with the exception of The Netherlands and Italy, where they are staff members in respectively about three-quarters and half of the settings; they are team members in only 20 per cent of the settings in Austria, Poland and Belgium, and their presence is almost negligible in Sweden, Finland, Denmark, Czechoslovakia, the UK and Switzerland, where they appear to be staff members in less than 5 per cent of the cases. In contrast to the early days of cardiac rehabilitation, there seem to be no psychiatrists involved in cardiac rehabilitation today in any country. If psychologists and social workers are thought to be the main agents of psychosocial care, it is clear that, with perhaps one exception, they are largely underrepresented on the European scene in comparison to medical and paramedical personnel.

Psychology and psychosocial care in cardiac rehabilitation

While the previous question already provided some information about the number of psychologists involved in cardiac rehabilitation after dismissal from the hospital, the questionnaire also included a more direct question concerning the involvement of psychologists in cardiac rehabilitation in general. The answers to this question showed important differences between European countries, ranging from a recognizable representation in Italy, Austria and The Netherlands, where between three and six psychologists are involved in cardiac rehabilitation per one million inhabitants, to a low representation in Belgium, Finland and Norway, where only one to three psychologists per one million inhabitants seem to be involved, to very low numbers in Switzerland, Poland, Czechoslovakia, Denmark, Ireland, Sweden and the UK, where fewer than one psychologist per one million inhabitants play a role in cardiac rehabilitation. If one realizes that their involvement may even be part-time in many cases, it is quite clear that the number of psychologists who are active in this domain does not reflect the considerable attention paid to psychological interventions in coronary heart disease in the literature (Bundy, 1989). Of course, this does not imply that no form of psychosocial intervention is offered in most European countries, since other professionals (e.g. nurses) can also play an important role in psychosocial care.

As a consequence, we also asked the respondents to indicate what percentage of cardiac rehabilitation patients are offered any form of psychosocial care after dismissal from the hospital. With the exception of Italy and Finland, where virtually all patients seem to get some form of psychosocial care, and Switzerland and Austria, where 40 to 60 per cent of patients receive some form of psychosocial care, psychosocial care seems to be offered in all other countries to less than 20 per cent of patients. It should be noted that in the case of Finland it appears as if psychosocial care is meant to compensate for the absence of exercise-based programmes. In addition, when these data are combined with the answers to the previous questions, it is obvious that, with the exception of Italy, Austria, The Netherlands and Finland, psychologists do not play a substantial role in the provision of psychosocial care to cardiac patients.

In order to get an idea of the kind of psychosocial care offered, we asked the respondents to what extent psychosocial care could be characterized as individual as opposed to group interventions and in what percentage of the cases partners were involved. With the exception of Denmark, Italy and Sweden, where group interventions seem to be more popular than individual interventions, over three-quarters of the psychosocial interventions can be characterized as individual in all other countries. In addition, it should be noted that psychosocial interventions in Denmark are not offered in hospital settings, but by the Danish Heart Association outside the hospital, while in Italy a more or less standard psychosocial group procedure consisting of two to three sessions is offered to the large majority of patients. Partners seemed to be involved in virtually all cases in Denmark and in about half of the cases in The Netherlands, Belgium, Sweden and the UK, but in all other countries their involvement is the exception rather than the rule.

A last question was concerned with various forms of psychosocial care, including interventions which focus on health education and the modification of life-styles; counselling for problems in daily life and stress management; psychotherapy; and a combination of any of these forms. In most countries, with the exception of the UK, Ireland, Denmark and Austria, a combination of these forms is most frequently offered, while forms of psychotherapy directed at changing personality characteristics related to coronary artery disease do not seem to be very popular in any country. Of the remaining two types of intervention, with the exception of the UK and Italy, counselling for daily life problems and stress management appears to be more frequently offered to cardiac patients than health education including life-style modification. This may illustrate that, with the exception of the UK, psychosocial interventions in Europe focus on psychosocial recovery and stress reduction rather than on life-style modification or secondary prevention.

Conclusions and discussion

While the present objectives of cardiac rehabilitation include psychosocial recovery (restoration of everyday behaviour) and secondary prevention (modification of specific life-styles), the effects of the traditional exercise-based cardiac rehabilitation programmes, at least in this respect, are quite modest.

As psychology can be defined as the science of behaviour and behavioural change, psychological interventions may affect these targets more easily. From this perspective there are at least two avenues for psychologists with respect to cardiac rehabilitation. The first is to improve the communication and intervention skills of other professionals. This can be done by increasing skills training in medical or paramedical education, and by in-service training. The second avenue is to add psychologists to the rehabilitation teams in order to develop systematic forms of psychological intervention, which could then be offered to large groups of patients and their partners. As there is evidence from controlled studies that both strategies will not only have beneficial effects on psychosocial recovery and compliance with medical advice but will also reduce cardiovascular morbidity and mortality, one may expect that psychologists will become at least part-time members of most cardiac rehabilitation teams in European countries.

In order to get an impression of the position of psychologists and the share of psychosocial care in cardiac rehabilitation in Europe, a questionnaire was sent out to two or three individuals in each European country. Health care professionals from 16 European countries returned their completed questionnaires on time. While such an approach did not provide us with detailed or perfectly reliable information, some interesting trends did emerge. For example, the results show that in general social workers and psychologists, who may be considered the main potential agents for psychosocial care, are largely underrepresented in cardiac rehabilitation teams.

As far as psychologists are concerned, the number involved in cardiac rehabilitation varies significantly from country to country. Three groups of countries could be distinguished: a group consisting of The Netherlands, Austria, and Italy, where psychologists are fairly well represented; a second one consisting of Norway, Finland and Belgium, where small numbers of psychologists are involved in cardiac rehabilitation; and a third group (the largest) consisting of Switzerland, Poland, Czechoslovakia, Denmark, Ireland, Sweden, the UK, Greece, Portugal and Turkey, where the number of psychologists is negligible.

Furthermore, there are only four countries where more than 20 per cent of patients receive a specific form of psychosocial care in addition to standard medical care and physical exercise training: Italy, Finland, Austria and Switzerland. In most other countries only a minority of the patients are offered psychosocial care. This should not always be seen as a lack of psychosocial intervention (as may in fact be the case in Czechoslovakia and Ireland). As the results of the survey show that most interventions are directed towards individual patients, this probably implies that in many countries much is done for a relatively small number of patients. This is in contrast to results from the research literature which suggest that larger groups of patients should be offered more systematic forms of intervention.

It is also remarkable that in some countries, such as Austria, Czechoslovakia, Finland, Italy and Poland, partners are seldom involved in psychosocial interventions, while they are at best involved in only about half of the cases in The Netherlands, Belgium, Sweden and the UK. This is in contrast to research findings which show that psychosocial recovery and patients' compliance is related to partners' support, and that family problems are an important reason for dropping out of rehabilitation programmes (Shanfield, 1990). While in many countries the most prevalent form of psychological intervention can be characterized as a combination of health education, counselling and stress management, it appears that counselling and stress management are probably the most common ingredients of psychosocial interventions. From a secondary prevention point of view, psychosocial professionals should also devote more attention and time to health education aimed at the modification of specific life-styles, including smoking, diet, excessive body weight, lack of physical exercise and alcohol abuse (Maes & van Veldhoven, 1990).

While many psychologists may be of the opinion that psychosocial care should be offered to every patient during cardiac rehabilitation, such a point of view is probably not realistic and not even defendable. It is obvious that, as is also the case for exercise-based forms of rehabilitation, some patients profit more than others from psychosocial intervention. Identifying these groups in future research and consequently developing screening measures for referral to psychosocial care would certainly support the claim of psychologists that psychosocial care in cardiac rehabilitation is both necessary and effective!

References

Bär, F. W., Cluitmans, J., Elderen, T. van, Maes, S., Rutten, F., Soons, P. & Stiggelbout, W. (1990). *Hartrevalidatie op maat, nieuwe visies*. (Cardiac rehabilitation to size, new ideas.) Report of the Rehabilitation Committee of the Dutch Heart Foundation. The Hague: Dutch Heart Foundation.

Bär, F. W. & Vonken, H. J. M. (1990). Wat is het nut van hartrevalidatie? (What are the effects of cardiac rehabilitation?) *Nederlands Tijdschrift voor Geneeskunde*, **134**, 107–112.

Bundy, C. (1989). Cardiac disorders. In A. K. Broome (Ed.), *Health Psychology: Processes and Applications*. New York: Chapman & Hall.

Burling, T. A., Singleton, E. G., Bigelow, G. E., Baile, W. F. & Gottlieb, S. W. (1984). Smoking following myocardial infarction: A critical review of the literature. *Health Psychology*, **3**, 83–96.

Davidson, C., Green, V. & Stansfield, B. (1988). Cardiac Rehabilitation in the United Kingdom 1985/86: A Questionnaire Survey. *Physiotherapy*, **8**.

Diederiks, J. P. M. (1982). Herstel en revalidatie na het hartinfarct. Deel I: Aard en omvang van het probleem (Cardiac recovery and rehabilitation. Part I: Nature and extent of the problem.) *Keesing Medisch Archief*, **1788**, 12271–12284.

Dishman, R. K., Sallis, J. F. & Orenstein, D. R. (1985). The determinants of physical activity and exercise. *Public Health Reports*, **100**, 158–171.

Dixhoorn, J. van (1991). *Relaxation Therapy in Cardiac Rehabilitation*. Doctoral dissertation. Erasmus University Rotterdam, The Netherlands.

Elderen, T. van (1991). *Health Education in Cardiac Rehabilitation*. Leiden: DSWO Press.

Erdman, R. A. M., Duivenvoorden, H. J., Verhage, F., Kazemier, M. & Hugenholtz, P. G. (1984). Hartrevalidatie: Een vervolgonderzoek over 5 jaar naar psychisch functioneren, werkhervatting, rookgewoonten en sportieve activiteiten (Cardiac rehabilitation: A 5-year follow-up study of psychological functioning, re-employment, smoking habits and sportive activities.) *Nederlands Tijdschrift voor de Geneeskunde*, **128**, 846–851.

Heller, S. S., Frank, K. A., Kornfeld, D. S., Wilson, S. N. & Malm, J. R. (1982). Psychological and behavioral responses following coronary artery bypass surgery. In Becker *et al.* (Eds), *Psychopathological and Neurological Dysfunctions Following Open Heart Surgery.* Berlin, Heidelberg: Springer Verlag.

Kallio, V., Hämäläinen, H., Hakkila, J. & Luurile, O. J. (1979). Reduction in sudden deaths by a multifactorial intervention programme after acute myocardial infarction. *Lancet*, **2**, 1091–1094.

Klapp, B. F. & Dahme, B. (1988). Die koronare Herzkrankheit – ein ganzheitlicher Prozess und die notwendige ganzheitliche Betrachtung dieser Krankheit. In B. F. Klapp & B. Dahme (Eds), *Psychosoziale Kardiologie* (Psychosocial Cardiology). Berlin: Springer.

Langosch, W. (1985). Behavioural interventions in cardiac rehabilitation. In A. Steptoe & A. Mathews (Eds), *Health Care and Human Behaviour.* London: Academic Press.

Leventhal, H., Prohaska, T. R. & Hirschman, R. S. (1985). Preventive health behaviour across the life span. In J. Rosen & L. Solomon (Eds), *Prevention in Health Psychology*, pp. 191–235. New York: University Press of New England.

Lipkin, D. P. (1991). Is cardiac rehabilitation necessary? *British Heart Journal*, **65**, 237–238.

Maes, S. & Elderen, T. van (1988). Effects of psycho-educational programmes in cardiac rehabilitation. *Netherlands Journal of Cardiology*, **1**, 30.

Maes, S., Elderen, T. van & Bruggemans, E. (1987). Effecten van voorlichting aan coronaire hartpatiënten. (Effects of health education for coronary heart patients.) *Gezondheid en Samenleving*, **2**, 60–76.

Maes, S., Foreest, M. van, Smulders, M., Elderen, T. van & Bruggemans, E. (1986). *Voorlichting aan coronaire hartpatienten (Health education for coronary heart patients.)* Een rapport in opdracht van het Ministerie van Welzijn, Volksgezondheid en Cultuur. (A report for the Dutch Ministry of Health.) Health Psychology Section, Tilburg University, The Netherlands.

Maes, S. & Veldhoven, M. van (1990). From health behaviour to health behaviour change. In A. A. Kaptein, H. M. van der Ploeg, B. Garssen, P. J. G. Schreurs & R. Beunderman (Eds), *Behavioural Medicine*, pp. 33–47. New York: Wiley.

Mulcahy, R. (1990). Cardiac rehabilitation. *Proceedings of the 5th European Regional Conference of Rehabilitation*, Dublin, Ireland, 20–25 May 1990.

O'Brien, (1984). Patterns of European Diagnoses and Prescribing, Office of Health Economics.

Oldridge, N. B., Guyatt, G. H., Fischer, M. E. & Rimm, A. A. (1988). Cardiac rehabilitation after myocardial infarction. Combined experience of randomized clinical trials. *Journal of the American Medical Association*, **260**, 945–950.

Organization for Economic Cooperation & Development. (1990). *Health Care Systems in Transition.* Paris: OECD.

Shanfield, S. B. (1990). Myocardial infarction and patients' wives. *Psychosomatics*, **31**, 138–145.

Soons, P. & Bär, F. (1990). Revalidatie van hartpatiënten tijdens opname en na ontslag uit het ziekenhuis: Cijfers en trends. (Rehabilitation of heart patients during and after hospital stay: Figures and trends.) *Nederlands Tijdschrift voor Geneeskunde*, **134**, 103–106.

Soons, P. & Bär, F. (1990). The present state of cardiac rehabilitation in The Netherlands. *Proceedings of the 5th European Regional Conference of Rehabilitation*, Dublin, Ireland, 20–25 May 1990.

World Health Organization (1989). *Statistics Annual.* Geneva: World Health Organization.

British Journal of Clinical Psychology (1992), **31**, 485–502   *Printed in Great Britain*
© 1992 The British Psychological Society

Cognitive predictors of health behaviour in contrasting regions of Europe*

Andrew Steptoe†

Department of Psychology, St George's Hospital Medical School, Cranmer Terrace, London SW17 0RE, UK

Jane Wardle†

ICRF Health Behaviour Unit, Institute of Psychiatry, De Crespigny Park, London SE5 8AF, UK

Four important health behaviours – dietary fat avoidance, regular exercise, smoking and alcohol consumption – were assessed by questionnaire, together with measures of risk awareness and beliefs about the importance of each behaviour for health, in comparable samples of young adults from eight countries: Belgium, England, Germany, Hungary, Ireland, Poland, Portugal and Spain. Results from 3223 men and 3930 women were analysed. Substantial differences in the prevalence of behaviours were identified, but no country consistently showed the most or least healthy profile across behaviours. Women tended to smoke and drink less than men and attempted to avoid dietary fat to a greater extent, while men exercised more than women. Ratings of the importance of behaviours for health were high, while risk awareness showed wide variations, with lower scores from samples in southern and eastern Europe. Across countries, few associations were observed between the prevalence of behaviour and either mean belief ratings or risk awareness. However, in comparisons of people who did and did not perform each behaviour, beliefs were consistently associated with practice. In multiple regression, beliefs about the importance of the behaviour for health independently accounted for 11.3 per cent of the variance in exercise, 18.9 per cent of the variance in smoking and 4.5 per cent of the variance in alcohol consumption. The association between beliefs and dietary fat avoidance was also substantial. In contrast, the relationships between risk awareness and behaviour were mixed. People who avoided dietary fat were more aware than others of the health risks of fat. But non-smokers were less aware than smokers of the risks of smoking, and people who drank regularly were more aware of the dangers of alcohol than were non-drinkers. The results are discussed in the context of the contribution of health psychology to European health promotion.

The principal causes of premature mortality in present-day Western countries are cancer, heart disease, and strokes. In 1987 these three conditions constituted over 65 per cent of causes of death in the US, compared with only 16 per cent in 1900 (Hinman, 1990). This increase is the more striking in view of the rise in prosperity and the improvements in medical care over this period. While the full aetiology of any of these diseases has yet to be understood, behavioural factors such as tobacco

---

* In accordance with Journal policy on submissions by editors and associate editors, editorial responsibility for this article was taken by Chris R. Brewin.
† Requests for reprints may be addressed to either author.

use, exercise, diet, alcohol consumption and preventive health checks are strongly implicated as risk factors (Amler & Dull, 1987). Consequently, the efforts of the public health movement have shifted from controlling exposure to infectious disease, which was the preoccupation of the first half of the 20th century, to modification of life-style. This has entailed a shift by public health physicians from collaboration with the purveyors of water supplies and sewerage, to new alliances with experts in human behaviour. Research into personal health behaviour is one of the most rapidly developing fields of psychology as researchers rise to the challenge of life-style modification (Rodin & Salovey, 1989; Taylor, 1991).

The geography of disease in Europe is attracting increasing attention in the light of the greater mobility within Europe, and the enactment in 1993 of the Single European Community Act. Tremendous variation in disease incidence and mortality across Europe has been identified (Holland, 1991). For example, coronary heart disease mortality among men aged 35–64 varied from less than 100/100 000 in France, Spain and Portugal to more than 300/100 000 in Czechoslovakia, Finland, Hungary, Ireland and Scotland. Stroke mortality in women aged 35–64 ranged from 12/100 000 in Switzerland to 74/100 000 in Hungary (WHO, 1989). Stomach cancer has been shown to be equally variable, going from an age-standardized mortality ratio of 13.1/100 000 in Greece to 35.8/100 000 in Poland in 1976 (Coggan & Acheson, 1984). The progressive reduction in trade, employment and training barriers across Europe is likely to have far-reaching effects in the health field. If these changes are to benefit the health as well as the economies of European countries, then attention must be paid to the factors which perpetuate the toll of premature mortality. The study of health behaviours across Europe is therefore of vital significance to the planning of preventive programmes.

Comparative behavioural studies across Europe are rare, although *per capita* figures for tobacco and alcohol use or food consumption have been used to indicate the considerable variation in behaviour. The relatively high fruit, vegetable and fish consumption and the comparatively low meat and fat intake in the Mediterranean countries, compared with central or northern Europe, has been implicated in the lower levels of heart disease and stroke (Buzina, Suboticanec & Saric, 1991). There is concern, however, that this diet may be compromised by increasing prosperity, since greater wealth has generally been shown to be associated with increases in meat and fat consumption (Trichopoulou & Efstathiadis, 1989). Tobacco consumption differences are also marked across Europe, ranging within the European Community from 47 per cent of the adult population in Denmark to 24 per cent in Portugal (EBASP, 1991 *a*). In view of the evidence of the linking of tobacco consumption to pricing (Townsend, 1990), the shift to equivalent levels of taxation across the European Community (CEC Directive COM(89)525final) could have serious health implications for countries such as the UK, which currently levy high taxes. Variations in activity and exercise have attracted little attention, perhaps because of the lack of *per capita* indices, although the Eurofit programme represents an attempt to develop a standardized assessment battery (Georgiades & Klissouras, 1989). However, in the Western world generally, the growing access to labour-saving devices, and more effective and affordable personal transport, has meant a reduction in activity. A shift to leisure-time energy expenditure is therefore necessary to achieve reasonable levels of fitness. This raises issues of accessibility and cost of appropriate facilities as well as the attitudes of the population. All of these considerations point to the need for regular surveillance of life-style to be given a priority at least equal to that of other aspects of the European environment, such as water quality or food labelling.

One of the major factors limiting accurate international comparisons of life-style factors is the absence of standardized measurements. An attempt to remedy this situation in relation to cardiovascular risk has been initiated with the MONICA project, although the main emphasis is on conventional risk factors such as serum lipids and blood pressure (WHO MONICA, 1989). The European Atherosclerosis Research Study (EARS) has obtained life-style data from young people in different regions of Europe, but results have not yet been reported. The WHO cross-national study of health behaviour in schoolchildren is one of the few cross-national behavioural studies in operation at present. It has identified substantial differences in smoking, exercise and drinking. For example 30 per cent of 15-year-old Finnish schoolboys reported smoking at least weekly compared with 17 per cent of Austrian schoolboys, and 32 per cent of Norwegian schoolgirls took regular exercise compared with 9 per cent of Welsh schoolgirls (Aarø, Wold, Kannas & Rimpela, 1986; Nutbeam, Aarø & Catford, 1989). A more recent survey of 11–15-year-old schoolchildren also reported marked differences across the EEC member states, with 49 per cent of Danes compared with 16 per cent of Italians having smoked (EBASP, 1991 *b*). Differences at this age could reflect the timing of smoking uptake, rather than final prevalence, but the MONICA project revealed major differences in smoking in adults, from 34 per cent of men in Northern Sweden to 63 per cent of men in Scotland (WHO MONICA, 1988).

Explanations for behavioural differences include a range of factors, from basic economic considerations to complex cultural influences, but it has been the individual cognitive factors, i.e. what people know or believe, which have attracted the attention of psychologists (Becker, 1974; Sejwacz, Ajzen & Fishbein, 1980). Knowledge about behaviour-health links (or risk awareness) is an essential factor in an informed choice concerning a healthy life-style. The role of smoking in causing lung cancer has been publicized widely, and the reduction in smoking over the past 20 years in the Western world can be attributed largely to the growing awareness of the serious health risks posed by tobacco use. However, the continuing high levels of tobacco use among lower socio-economic status groups, and the growing uptake of smoking among adolescent girls in some countries, illustrate the fact that knowledge of health risks is not a sufficient condition for avoidance of smoking. Similarly, few adults in the UK can be unaware that sweets promote dental disease, or that a high fat diet can increase the risk of heart disease; nevertheless, sugar and fat consumption over the past decade have scarcely shown any change (*The Health of the Nation*, 1991).

Another cognitive factor which is closely allied with risk awareness is belief or attitude. Almost all accounts of health behaviour incorporate some concept which addresses the individual's belief in the value of the behaviour (Becker, 1974; Rogers, 1983; Weinstein 1988). Few studies fail to find a relationship between aspects of evaluation and behaviour. For example, the estimated value of breast self-examination

Andrew Steptoe and Jane Wardle

predicts frequency, belief in the utility of teaching children about safety predicts parents' efforts to teach this to their children, and the perceived advantages of sunscreens in preventing skin cancer are associated with sunscreen use (Calnan, 1984; Cody & Lee, 1990; Peterson, Farmer & Kashani, 1990).

The predictive power of cognitive variables has varied across studies, with some identifying strong differences in behaviour between groups who differ in their attitudes, while others find relatively small effects (Davidson & Jaccard, 1979; Heberlein & Black, 1976). The methods of measurement and specificity of items selected contribute to this variation, with stronger effects when the attitudes and behaviour are measured at similar levels of generality. Differences also emerge between behaviours, relating to the lesser contribution of beliefs compared with other determinants such as habit in some domains (Sutton & Eiser, 1990). However, few studies have used identical methods, in samples from different backgrounds, in order to establish whether the cognitive determinants survive differences in the prevalence of the behaviour.

The present paper addresses these issues by comparing the predictive power of the cognitive factors across European countries which vary in their patterns of health behaviour. Data are drawn from the European Health and Behaviour Survey, one of the first studies to attempt concurrent recording of behaviours and cognitive variables. It was based on the use of a common assessment protocol which was translated and back-translated into 15 languages, with a standardized scoring and data management system (Wardle & Steptoe, 1991). Data have been collected from target samples of 800 university students from 20 countries. A range of health-related behaviours were sampled, along with associated beliefs and risk-factor knowledge. Data were also collected on health status and current medical treatment, as well as a number of psychosocial variables such as health-related locus of control, the perceived value of health, social support and depression.

This analysis is based on data collected in eight countries selected to represent the diverse cultures of Europe across well-established geographical axes, including eastern Europe (Hungary, Poland), the Mediterranean (Portugal, Spain), central Europe (Belgium, Germany) and the British Isles (England, Ireland). Data related to four major health behaviours – the avoidance of dietary fat, regular exercise, cigarette smoking and alcohol consumption – are discussed, together with associated attitudes and beliefs. This analysis has three main aims:

1. to determine whether there are important differences in the prevalence of these four health behaviours in comparable groups of healthy young adults from different parts of Europe;
2. to establish whether beliefs about health benefit and risk awareness show a similar distribution to health behaviours;
3. to investigate the interrelationships between cognitive and behavioural variables across contrasting European countries.

Method

Full details of the European Health and Behaviour Survey are given elsewhere (Wardle & Steptoe 1991), and only the items included in the present analysis will be described here.

Subjects and procedure

Data were collected from 7153 students aged 17–30 from eight countries as detailed in Table 1. Within each country, the data were collected from students in the following places: Diepenbeek (Belgium), London area and Bath (England), Hamburg and Wuppertal (West Germany), Budapest (Hungary), Dublin (Ireland), Bytom and Kracow (Poland), Lisbon (Portugal) and Granada (Spain). None of the participants were studying health-related courses. Subjects completed the survey in classes. They were told that the survey concerned activities related to health and that an international comparison was being carried out, but no further details were provided. They were assured of complete anonymity. Administration of the survey in classes allowed failures of completion to be counted accurately. The protocol was completed by 90–100 per cent of the various classes approached.

Health behaviour

Conscious efforts to avoid fat and cholesterol in the diet were assessed on a *Yes/No* format. Physical activity was assessed by questions concerning exercise over the last two weeks, the type of exercise, and the number of sessions carried out. Three categories of exercise were derived from this information – none, one to four sessions in the past 14 days, and five or more sessions. Smoking was assessed with eight response options that were subsequently reduced to four categories: no smoking, fewer than one cigarette per day, 1–10 per day, 10 or more per day. Alcohol consumption was measured by asking subjects which of the following terms best described them: non-drinker, special occasions drinker, occasional and regular drinker. Occasional and regular drinkers were asked on how many days over the last two weeks they had had a drink, and how many drinks they had consumed on those days. These data were used to derive four categories of alcohol consumption: none, very occasional, fewer than one drink per day, and more than one drink per day over the past 14 days.

Beliefs in health benefits

Participants were asked to rate the importance of a series of behaviours for health maintenance on 10-point scales, where 1 = low importance and 10 = very great importance to health. Four items were included in this analysis: Beliefs in not eating too much fat, taking regular exercise, not smoking, and not drinking too much alcohol.

Risk appraisal

The risk-knowledge items involved asking the subjects to indicate whether or not each of dietary fat, exercise, smoking and alcohol consumption contributed to five different health problems (heart disease, lung cancer, mental illness, breast cancer, high blood pressure). The same items were presented to a panel of experienced epidemiologists and public health researchers from different parts of Europe in order to establish which links are currently accepted by authorities. A risk-awareness index was calculated for each behaviour based on the associations endorsed by the expert panel. For the avoidance of dietary fat and cholesterol, associations with heart disease and breast cancer were accepted. The scores for an individual could therefore range between 0 and 2. Exercise was considered to be associated with heart disease and high blood pressure (range 0–2), smoking with heart disease, lung cancer and high blood pressure (range 0–3) and alcohol with heart disease and high blood pressure (range 0–2).

Health status

Health status is consistently found to be related to health behaviours (Belloc & Breslow, 1972; Gottlieb & Green, 1984). Students were deliberately targeted in this study in order to reduce the variance attributable to health status, but it is nevertheless possible that small variations might contribute to the pattern of results. Four measures were therefore included to assess health status. Subjects were asked whether they suffered from any persistent health problems, whether they had received treatment from a doctor over the past month, and whether they had used prescribed or unprescribed (over the counter) medications over the past month. If any of these questions were positively endorsed, the respondent was asked for details. Most health problems were of a trivial nature, such as skin complaints or flu. In the present analyses, the four measures of health status were included in a binary *Yes/No* format.

Analysis

The frequency of health behaviours, belief and risk awareness in the eight countries was compared using χ^2 statistics and analysis of variance as appropriate. *Post hoc* comparisons following significant main effects in analysis of variance were assessed using Tukey's HSD test. The associations between behaviour, beliefs and risk awareness were analysed in a series of hierarchical multiple regressions in the case of exercise, smoking and alcohol consumption, and by hierarchical logistic regression for the avoidance of fat and cholesterol. In each analysis, the behaviour was the dependent variable. Sex and age were entered at the first stage, followed by the four health status indices at the second stage. Risk awareness was entered third, and the appropriate belief measures was entered last.

Results

The characteristics of the sample are outlined in Table 1. The average ages of subjects completing the survey ranged from 18.5 years in Belgium to 23.5 years in Germany. The main effect for country was significant in the analysis of age ($p < .001$), and *post hoc* tests confirmed that each country differed from all others except for Hungary–Spain and Poland–Portugal.

Table 1. Sample characteristics

	Total number	Men	Women	Age mean (SD)
Belgium	1630	725	905	18.5 (1.4)
England	723	308	415	20.1 (2.5)
Germany	791	400	391	23.5 (2.6)
Hungary	757	377	380	20.9 (2.3)
Ireland	786	307	479	19.0 (1.9)
Poland	799	399	400	21.8 (2.1)
Portugal	856	332	524	22.1 (2.8)
Spain	811	375	436	20.8 (2.4)

Prevalence of health behaviours

The prevalence of the four behaviours in men and women from each country is summarized in Tables 2 and 3. The differences between countries were significant for all behaviours in both men and women, confirming the wide variation in the levels of healthy behaviour reported across these regions of Europe (all $\chi^2 > 26.5$, $p < .001$). For example, the proportion of people who had exercised over the past 14 days varied between 36 and 87.4 per cent for men, and 34 and 95 per cent for women. The proportion of non-smokers ranged across countries from 54.8 to 84.6 per cent for men and 59.3 to 87.6 per cent for women. No country sample consistently showed the most or least healthy pattern across behaviours. Thus among men, the countries in which fewest subjects exercised were Spain and Portugal, while the countries with the highest alcohol consumption were England and Ireland. Belgium had a favourable smoking profile, but was the country in which the fewest men attempted to avoid dietary fat.

Table 2. Prevalence of health behaviours in eight European countries. Men— Percentage endorsing each category

	Avoidance of fat and cholesterol		Exercise Sessions in the past 14 days			Cigarette smoking Cigarettes per day				Alcohol consumption Drinks per day over past 14 days			
	No	Yes	None	1–4	5+	None	< 1	1–10	10+	None	V.Occ	< 1	> 1
Belgium	78.8	21.2	20.2	33.4	46.4	82.9	3.3	8.5	5.3	19.2	32.7	17.6	30.5
England	67.5	32.5	32.2	36.9	30.9	69.9	11.1	10.5	8.5	14.8	19.0	29.2	37.0
Germany	64.7	35.3	23.2	35.5	41.2	59.2	8.8	11.3	20.7	12.3	16.7	45.1	25.9
Hungary	66.8	33.2	12.6	44.8	42.6	84.6	3.7	7.7	4.0	13.3	45.4	26.0	15.2
Ireland	69.6	30.4	27.0	31.1	41.6	73.9	8.5	6.9	10.8	10.9	11.9	40.1	37.1
Poland	75.3	24.7	25.3	46.2	28.5	65.3	5.8	13.1	15.8	13.2	37.3	31.9	17.6
Portugal	78.4	21.6	49.2	32.7	18.1	54.8	10.0	15.2	20.0	15.3	31.8	34.1	18.8
Spain	72.7	27.3	64.0	14.3	21.7	67.2	6.7	8.3	17.7	12.9	25.1	34.0	28.0

Table 3. Prevalence of health behaviours in eight European countries. Women— Percentage endorsing each category

	Avoidance of fat and cholesterol		Exercise Sessions in the past 14 days			Cigarette smoking Cigarettes per day				Alcohol consumption Drinks per day over past 14 days			
	No	Yes	None	1–4	5+	None	< 1	1–10	10+	None	V.Occ	< 1	> 1
Belgium	59.0	41.0	30.9	41.1	28.0	87.6	2.6	7.6	2.2	34.2	46.0	13.5	6.4
England	47.2	52.8	37.6	36.8	25.6	71.2	9.9	8.2	10.7	14.0	20.6	37.5	27.9
Germany	50.8	49.2	22.7	42.1	35.2	64.2	7.2	13.1	15.5	13.0	25.9	52.1	9.1
Hungary	55.9	44.1	5.0	62.0	33.1	84.9	2.1	9.3	3.7	16.7	61.5	16.1	5.7
Ireland	52.5	47.5	32.8	25.5	41.7	67.5	8.2	15.5	8.8	12.2	13.3	51.0	23.6
Poland	59.3	40.8	26.8	53.4	19.7	77.9	5.0	11.3	5.8	15.1	57.5	21.2	6.1
Portugal	58.1	41.9	66.0	24.4	9.6	59.3	6.3	19.8	14.6	25.3	51.7	17.9	5.1
Spain	52.2	47.8	40.9	31.0	28.0	63.0	6.2	17.3	13.4	18.2	40.3	30.5	11.0

There was however some consistency in the ranking of men and women from the same country. Hungarian men and women both showed high exercise and low smoking levels compared with other countries, while England and Ireland were at the top of the alcohol consumption league in both sexes. Sex differences in the prevalence of health behaviours were also relatively consistent across countries. In all eight countries, men drank more alcohol than women (all $\chi^2 > 8.40$, $p < .05$), while more women than men avoided fat and cholesterol (all $\chi^2 > 15.6$, $p < .001$). Five countries showed a significant sex difference in exercise, with men exercising more than women in each case (Belgium, Poland, Hungry, Portugal and Spain). The sex difference was also significant in five countries for cigarette smoking (Belgium, Ireland, Poland, Portugal and Spain), with more men than women smoking. Overall therefore, there was a tendency for women to be more health conscious than men in terms of diet, cigarette smoking and alcohol consumption, but for men to exercise more regularly.

Belief ratings

Mean ratings of the beliefs of the importance of the four behaviours for health maintenance are shown in Table 4. The differences between countries in ratings are significant for all four scales in both sexes ($p < .001$). Age differences between countries were taken account of by including age as a covariate in the analyses. *Post hoc* comparisons indicated that among men, the Hungarian sample had relatively high ratings of the importance of exercise and not smoking, and low ratings for the avoidance of fat. Both Hungarian and Polish men rated moderation in alcohol intake highly and fat avoidance relatively low. Among women, ratings of the importance of avoiding fat were low in the Belgian and Hungarian samples (with significant differences from all other countries), while German and English women rated moderation in alcohol consumption as less important than did all others ($p < .05$). Sex differences in belief ratings were rather uniform across countries. In all eight cases, women rated fat avoidance and moderation in alcohol consumption as more important than did men ($p < .001$). No significant sex differences were observed in beliefs about regular exercise, except in Spain ($p < .01$). The results for smoking were mixed, with women regarding not smoking as more important for health than men in Belgium, Poland and Portugal, but with no sex differences in the other five countries.

Table 4. Beliefs in importance of behaviours for health maintenance. Mean ratings (1–10 scale) in men and women from eight European countries

Beliefs in:	Not eating too much fat		Taking regular exercise		Not smoking		Not drinking too much alcohol	
	Men	Women	Men	Women	Men	Women	Men	Women
Belgium	4.87	6.33	7.81	7.84	8.26	8.91	6.81	7.74
England	6.21	7.11	8.04	7.92	8.24	8.45	6.39	7.21
Germany	6.54	7.41	8.23	8.16	7.93	8.21	6.54	6.86
Hungary	5.35	6.27	8.97	9.15	8.96	9.01	7.69	8.15
Ireland	6.05	7.24	8.37	8.19	8.43	8.52	6.88	7.80
Poland	5.58	7.22	7.66	7.76	8.00	8.81	7.49	8.23
Portugal	6.40	7.64	8.31	8.13	8.05	8.58	6.78	7.79
Spain	6.07	7.12	8.37	7.97	8.38	8.50	6.70	7.70

The question of whether variations in the prevalence of healthy behaviour across countries were associated with the level of belief in the importance of that behaviour for health maintenance was analysed using product moment correlations across the eight countries. The correlation between the proportion of people in the country avoiding fat and level of belief in fat avoidance was not significant for men or women ($r = -.39$ and $-.25$ respectively). Similarly, the proportion of exercisers was not correlated with the average ratings of the importance of exercise. But in the case of smoking, correlations were significant for both men and women ($r = .77$ and $.82$ respectively, $p < .01$). The proportion of non-smokers in each country was positively associated with the mean rating of the importance of not smoking. For men but not women the number of subjects consuming one or more drinks on average during the last 14 days was negatively correlated with mean belief ratings across countries (men: $r = -.72$, $p < .05$; women: $r = -.39$, n.s.).

Risk awareness

Table 5 summarizes the risk awareness scores associated with each of the health behaviours. Country differences controlling for age were significant on all four behaviours for men and women ($p < .001$). *Post hoc* tests using Tukey's HSD indicated that for awareness of the diseases associated with dietary fat, Polish men and women scored below other countries, while the awareness levels in the English and Irish samples were high. In relation to the awareness of risks associated with lack of exercise, Poland, Belgium and Portugal scored below the other five countries, none of whom differed from one another. The Polish and Belgian samples were again poorly informed about the diseases associated with smoking in comparison with others, while the German and English samples had high scores. The samples from Hungary, Poland and Portugal were significantly less well informed about the risks

Table 5. Risk awareness – Role of behaviours in disease. Mean levels of risk awareness in eight European countries

Awareness of risk associated with:	Dietary fat (0–2)		Lack of exercise (0–2)		Cigarette smoking (0–3)		Alcohol consumption (0–2)	
	Men	Women	Men	Women	Men	Women	Men	Women
Belgium	.76	.70	.64	.66	1.74	1.72	1.01	1.11
England	.91	.96	.97	1.07	2.11	2.18	1.17	1.30
Germany	.83	.76	1.11	1.07	2.25	2.10	1.33	1.34
Hungary	.72	.66	.98	.94	1.94	1.89	.91	.92
Ireland	.90	.93	1.09	.97	2.15	1.88	1.25	1.22
Poland	.63	.62	.58	.55	1.62	1.43	1.01	.92
Portugal	.75	.72	.67	.71	1.95	1.82	.93	.99
Spain	.81	.78	.87	.82	2.04	1.83	1.21	1.15

of alcohol than were the German, English, Irish and Spanish men and women ($p < .05$).

There were few significant sex differences in risk awareness. However, the mean awareness score for cigarette smoking was significantly higher for men than for women in five countries (Germany, Ireland, Poland, Portugal and Spain, $p < .05$). It is interesting that in three of these countries (Poland, Portugal and Spain), smoking was more prevalent among men than women, suggesting that the awareness of risks associated with tobacco does not necessarily lead to low consumption.

Correlations between the prevalence of health behaviour and mean risk awareness levels were calculated across countries. Effects were not significant for exercise or smoking. Among women, countries in which awareness of the risk of dietary fat was high tended to show more avoidance of fat and cholesterol, but the relationship was less strong for men (women: $r = -.82$, $p < .01$; men: $r = -.48$, n.s.). Significant correlations between alcohol consumption and awareness of alcohol risks were observed in both men and women ($r = .67$ and $.66$ respectively. $p < .05$). However, high risk awareness scores were recorded in national samples with high alcohol consumption levels, contrary to the notion that more alcohol would be consumed in populations who were ill informed about the dangers of excessive drinking.

Predictors of health behaviour

A series of hierarchical multiple regressions were performed on exercise, cigarette smoking and alcohol consumption in order to identify the independent predictors of behaviour. These analyses were carried out separately for each country, and also for the entire sample combined. Since results were comparable across countries, only the combined models will be presented.

In the multiple regression on exercise behaviour, sex and age emerged as independent predictors ($\beta = -.118$ and $-.111$, $t = -10.3$ and -9.69, respectively, $p < .0001$). Exercise was less frequent among older subjects, an effect that was significant in three of the individual country analyses (Belgium, Hungary and Poland). Men exercised more than women overall, as noted earlier. The health status measures and risk awareness were not associated with exercise. The most powerful independent predictor was belief in the importance of exercise for health ($\beta = .337$, $t = 29.6$, $p < .0001$). This effect is illustrated in Fig. 1, where the orderly relationship between behaviour and belief is evident. Beliefs in the importance of exercise accounted for 11.3 per cent of the variance in the overall model. In the separate analyses by country, beliefs independently accounted for 7.3 per cent (Hungary) to 15.7 per cent (Belgium) of the variance in exercise behaviour.

The analysis of smoking behaviour revealed age as an independent predictor in the overall model ($\beta = .161$, $t = 15.1$, $p < .0001$). Age was significant in six of the eight individual country analyses, as in each case, smokers tended to be older. Thus the mean age of non-smokers was 20.3 (SD 2.6), while that of subjects smoking 10 or more cigarettes per day was 22.0 (SD 3.0). Sex was not associated with smoking in the overall model, although, as noted previously, men smoked more than women in five countries. Subjects who had taken medication either from their doctors or over the counter over the last month were more likely to be smokers ($\beta = .022$ and $.021$,

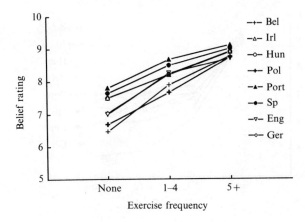

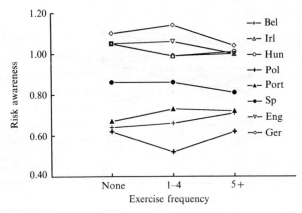

Figure 1. Mean ratings of belief in the benefits of exercise (upper panel) and awareness of risks associated with sedentary life-styles (lower panel) in subjects who had not exercised at all in the past two weeks (None), who had exercised 1–4 times, and 5 or more times (5+).

$t = 1.90$ and 1.95 respectively, $p < .05$). Both risk awareness ($\beta = .69$, $t = 6.50$, $p < .0001$) and belief in the importance of not smoking ($\beta = -.436$, $t = -41.2$, $p < .0001$) were independent predictors in the overall model, and these effects are plotted in Fig. 2. Risk awareness was positively associated with smoking, so smokers were more knowledgeable about the risks of smoking than were non-smokers. By contrast, beliefs were negatively associated with smoking, with non-smokers giving higher ratings of the importance of not smoking than did smokers. Beliefs were more important and robust independent predictors of smoking than was risk awareness. In the separate analyses by country, risk awareness was significant in five countries while beliefs were reliable predictors in all eight. Overall, the incremental variance accounted for by adding risk awareness to the model was only 0.34 per cent, while

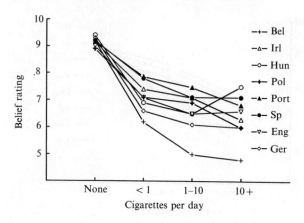

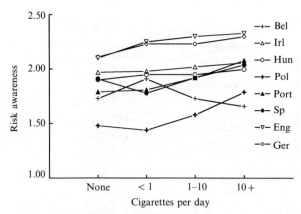

Figure 2. Mean ratings of belief in the importance of not smoking (upper panel) and awareness of the risks associated with smoking (lower panel) in non-smokers (None), and those who smoked fewer than 1 cigarette per day (< 1), 1–10 per day, and 10 or more per day (10+).

the additional variance attributable to beliefs was 18.9 percent. In the individual countries, beliefs accounted for 12.3 (Poland) to 28.3 per cent (Belgium) of the variance in cigarette smoking.

Both age and sex emerged as independent predictors of alcohol consumption (β = .57 and −.176, t = 4.94 and −14.8 respectively, $p <$ .0001). Men drank more than women (significantly more in all eight countries), while regular drinkers tended to be older than non-drinkers (significant in five countries). People who consumed alcohol were more likely to have taken physician-prescribed or over the counter medication over the last month than non-drinkers (β = .061 and .082, t = 4.81 and 6.77 respectively, $p <$ .0001). Both risk awareness (β = .075, t = 6.54, $p <$ .0001) and beliefs (β = −.215, t = −18.4, $p <$ .0001) again emerged as independent predictors, and their associations with alcohol consumption are shown in Fig. 3. The

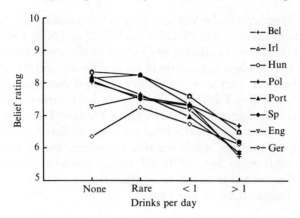

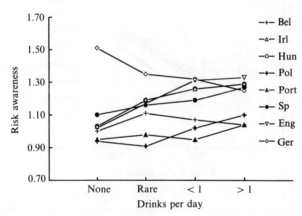

Figure 3. Mean ratings of belief in the importance of drinking only moderately (upper panel) and awareness of the diseases associated with alcohol (lower panel) in non-drinkers (None), very occasional drinkers (Rare), and subjects who had drunk fewer than one (< 1) or more than one (> 1) drink per day on average over the past two weeks.

more alcohol that subjects drank, the more aware they were of the health risk of drinking. This corroborates the correlation between risk awareness and the number of regular drinkers in each country that was described earlier. The effect was present in three countries in separate analyses, but was relatively small, accounting in the final model for only 0.53 per cent of the variance. The relationship between consumption and beliefs was more powerful, being reliable in seven of the eight individual country analyses, and overall accounting for 4.47 per cent of the variance.

The prediction of the avoidance of dietary fat was analysed by hierarchical logistic regression. Sex was a powerful predictor, with women being more likely to avoid fat than men (Wald = 66.4, Odds = 1.60, $p < .0001$). Three of the health status variables were associated with fat avoidance. In each case, subjects with a worse health status (those suffering from chronic problems, those who had recently received treatment from a doctor, and those who had taken non-prescribed medication) were more likely to be making efforts to eat healthily (Wald = 5.13, 7.32 and 3.75, Odds = 1.18, 1.21 and 1.12, $p < .05$). Both risk awareness and beliefs in the importance of not eating too much fat were independent predictors of fat avoidance, and the associations are plotted in Fig. 4. Subjects who avoided dietary fat were more aware of the health risks (Wald = 16.0, Odds = 1.26, $p < .0001$), and held firmer beliefs about the importance of controlling fat intake (Wald = 851.3, Odds = 1.45, $p < .0001$). Of the two, beliefs were most consistently associated with fat avoidance, since the effect was significant in all eight countries, while for risk awareness, the effect was significant in only one. The odds ratio for the belief rating indicates that for every unit increment on the 10-point belief rating scale, the odds of a subject avoiding dietary fat and cholesterol increased by 45 per cent.

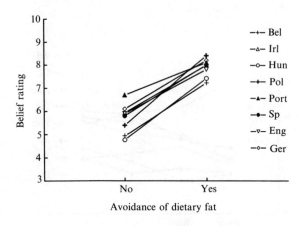

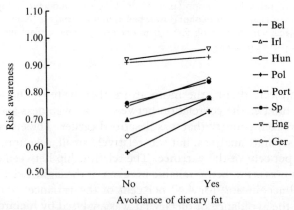

Figure 4. Mean ratings of beliefs in not eating too much fat (upper panel) and awareness of the risks associated with dietary fat consumption (lower panel) in subjects who do (Yes) and do not (No) make conscious efforts to avoid fat and cholesterol in the diet.

Discussion

This paper reports an interim analysis of data collected in the European Health and Behaviour Survey. Information was collected about personal health behaviours from students using a standard questionnaire. The reasons for studying students have been outlined elsewhere, but the following considerations were important (see Wardle & Steptoe, 1991). Firstly, the prevention of serious illnesses such as coronary heart disease and cancer begins early in life; secondly, the comparison of life-style factors across Europe is only possible if similar people are assessed in each country, and students represent a homogeneous and easily identifiable group; thirdly, the administration of the survey in classes ensured a high response rate, reducing the biases that might arise through selection. Caution must be exercised in the interpretation of questionnaire data, and it is likely that some respondents represented their life-styles as more healthy than is objectively the case. However, there is no reason to suppose any systematic variation in bias across different parts of Europe.

The data concerning diet, exercise, smoking and alcohol consumption reveal a marked split between recommendations concerning health behaviour and the reported health practices of the young, well-educated subjects who took part in the survey. Among the men, fewer than one-third made any effort to avoid dietary fat, only about one-third took regular exercise, nearly 30 per cent were smokers and more than a quarter were drinking alcohol daily. Women showed 'healthier' behaviour patterns than men, with higher levels of fat avoidance, and lower consumption of cigarettes and alcohol, although they took even less exercise.

Considerable variation across countries was seen for all four areas of behaviour sampled. These were very similar for men and women. Although age was a significant predictor of three out of the four behaviours, the age differences between countries did not account for the variation in prevalence of the behaviours. No one country stood out as especially 'healthy' or 'unhealthy' across the board, although the Hungarians were among the top two most healthy for all four behaviours in the men, and for two of the four in women. Portugal was likewise near the bottom for three out of four behaviours in the men and two out of four in the women. Analysis by broader geographical region (eastern versus western Europe or northern versus southern Europe) failed to support the utility of these axes in predicting health behaviour, suggesting that cultural rather than geographical factors are influential on personal health behaviours.

Assessment of beliefs about the importance of behaviour to health revealed that subjects were broadly convinced that life-style was relevant to health. Not smoking and taking regular exercise were rated overall as more important than moderating alcohol consumption, which was in turn rated more important than avoiding dietary fat. This pattern was seen in both men and women. There were considerable differences between countries, but no clear trends for one country to endorse all four behaviours more strongly than others. As with the behaviours, women revealed a 'healthier' belief profile than men except in the domain of exercise, which women rated *less* important than men.

Risk awareness was measured in a straightforward fashion, relying on *Yes/No* indications of relationships between behaviour and specific illnesses. Methods such as this make for ease of completion but are likely to overestimate subjects' risk awareness. Nevertheless, the proportion of subjects endorsing the links which have received unqualified acceptance scientifically (such as smoking and heart disease) fell well short of 100 per cent. Participants from eastern Europe, the Mediterranean countries and Belgium identified fewer than half of the established links. The sex differences favouring women that had emerged in beliefs and behaviours were not identified in risk awareness. Women had higher scores than men overall in two countries and men higher than women in five countries.

Interrelationships between cognitive and behavioural variables revealed interesting patterns. Analyses across countries explored the extent to which the prevalence of each behaviour was associated with average levels of belief and risk awareness. Few effects were identified for beliefs; thus differences in fat intake, exercise and alcohol consumption across countries were not paralleled by beliefs in the importance of these factors. Nevertheless, in the case of smoking, what might be termed 'national levels of belief' were associated with behaviour, so that countries rating not smoking as more important tended to have fewer smokers. The analogous analyses of risk awareness showed no significant associations for either exercise or smoking. The cross-country correlation between risk awareness and alcohol consumption was significant, but contradictory to the simple notion that drinking would be less prevalent in countries where health risks are better known.

The influence of these cognitive variables was more powerful when comparisons were made either within countries, or across the entire sample, between people at different levels of each health behaviour. The most consistent predictor of each of the four behaviours was the corresponding belief rating. In each case, people who behaved in a more 'healthy' fashion had firmer beliefs in the importance of the behaviour for health maintenance than did others. Figures 1–4 show a striking overlap in the associations of beliefs and behaviours in different countries, despite the wide cultural variations, attesting to the robustness of this finding. In hierarchical regression, the variance in behaviour accounted for by beliefs after demographic factors, health status and risk awareness had been taken into consideration ranged from 18.9 per cent for smoking to 4.5 per cent for alcohol consumption. These results are consistent with many other studies showing that beliefs in the value of preventive action are associated with the probability that the action is performed (e.g. Biddle & Ashford, 1988; Calnan & Rutter, 1988; Terry, Oakland & Ankeny, 1991).

The findings on the relationship between risk awareness and health behaviour are less straightforward. Knowledge about the relevance of life-style factors for health is an important preliminary to health promotion and behaviour change (see Nutbeam *et al.*, 1989). A simple model would predict that risk awareness is greater among people practising the healthy option. In fact, this pattern was observed only for dietary fat avoidance, in that subjects who avoided fat had significantly higher risk awareness scores (Fig. 4). No association between risk awareness and exercise behaviour was seen. The data plotted in Fig. 1 show that the awareness of the risks associated with sedentary life-styles varies across countries, but is not generally higher among regular exercisers. The results for smoking and alcohol consumption are striking in showing significant inverse associations between risk awareness and behaviour (Fig. 2 and 3). These effects indicate that subjects who smoke or drink regularly are more rather than less aware of the risks associated with the behaviour. Inconsistencies in the relationship between risk awareness and personal health behaviour are found elsewhere in the literature (Nutbeam *et al.*, 1989; Shewry, Smith & Tunstall-Pedoe, 1990). The observation of an inverse association may reflect our assessment of a relatively well-educated group. Well-educated smokers and drinkers may indeed be better informed than others about the risks associated with their habits, while in the broader spectrum of the population, ignorance may be a more important factor.

The use of samples of similar social and educational background across countries, which nevertheless differed in terms of health beliefs and health behaviour, permitted a careful analysis of the links between cognition and behaviour. The results confirmed strong links between beliefs and behaviour, although in the present data set it was not possible to determine whether beliefs regulated behaviour, or behaviour determined beliefs. Risk awareness showed a much more complex pattern, indicating that knowledge was not a deterrent to smoking or drinking nor a promoter of exercise. The results support the approach of combining assessments of cognitive factors with measures of life-style in attempting to understand patterns of health behaviour. The striking contrasts between different countries of Europe emphasize that research conducted in one region may not generalize well to other parts of Europe, and that international comparisons are essential if scientifically based prevention policies are to be generated that are applicable throughout the continent.

Acknowledgements

This research was carried out within the Concerted Action on Breakdown in Human Adaptation: Quantification of Parameters, part of the Commission of the European Communities Medical and Health Research Programme. The following participants in the European Health and Behaviour Survey contributed to the work described in this paper: Drs Andrzej Brodziak, Ray Fuller, Joao Justo, Maria Kopp, Gudrun Sartory, Arpad Skrabski, Jaime Vila, Jan Vinck and Zbigniew Zarczynski.

References

Aarø, L. E., Wold, B., Kannas, L. & Rimpela, M. (1986). Health behaviour in schoolchildren: A WHO cross-national survey. A presentation of philosophy, methods and selected results of the first survey. *Health Promotion*, **1**, 17–33.

Amler, R. W. & Dull, H. B. (1987). *Closing the Gap*. New York: Oxford University Press.

Becker, M. H. (Ed.) (1974). The health belief model and personal health behavior. *Health Education Monographs*, **2**, 324–508.

Belloc, N. B. & Breslow, L. (1972). Relationship of physical health status and health practices. *Preventive Medicine*, **1**, 409–421.

Biddle, S. & Ashford, B. (1988). Cognitions and perceptions of health and exercise. *British Journal of Sports Medicine*, **22**, 135–140.

Buzina, R., Suboticanec, K. & Saric, M. (1991). Diet and health problems: Diet in Southern Europe. *Annual Review of Metabolism*, **35**, 32–40.

Calnan, M. (1984). The health belief model and participation in programmes for the early detection of breast cancer: A comparative analysis. *Social Science and Medicine*, **19**, 823–830.

Calnan, M. & Rutter, D. R. (1988). Do health beliefs predict health behaviour: A follow-up analysis of breast self-examination. *Social Science and Medicine*, **24**, 463–465.

Cody, R. & Lee, C. (1990). Behaviors, beliefs, and intentions in skin cancer prevention. *Journal of Behavioral Medicine*, **13**, 373–389.

Coggan, D. & Acheson, E. D. (1984). The geography of cancer of the stomach. *British Medical Bulletin*, **40**, 335–341.

Davidson, A. R. & Jaccard, J. J. (1979). Variables that moderate the attitude–behavior relation: Results of a longitudinal survey. *Journal of Personality and Social Psychology*, **37**, 1364–1376.

European Bureau for Action on Smoking Prevention (1991 *a*). Percentage of smokers in the EC. *Newsletter*, **13**, 11.

European Bureau for Action on Smoking Prevention (1991 *b*). Young Europeans, tobacco and alcohol. *Newsletter*, **11**, 9–11.

Georgiades, G. & Klissouras, V. (1989). Assessment of youth fitness: The European perspective. *American Journal of Clinical Nutrition*, **49**, 1048–1853.

Gottlieb, N. H. & Green, L. W. (1984). Life events, social network, life-style and health: an analysis of the 1979 National Survey of Personal Health Practices and Consequences. *Health Education Quarterly*, **11**, 91–105.

Heberlein, T. A. & Black, J. S. (1976). Attitudinal specificity and the prediction of behavior in a field study. *Journal of Personality and Social Psychology*, **33**, 474–479.

Hinman, A. R. (1990). 1889 to 1989: A century of health and disease. *Public Health Reports*, **105**, 374–380.

Holland, W. W. (Ed.). (1991). *European Community Atlas of 'Avoidable Death'*, 2nd ed. Oxford: Oxford University Press.

Nutbeam, D., Aarø, L. E. & Catford, J. (1989). Understanding children's health behaviour: The implications for health promotion for young people. *Social Science and Medicine*, **29**, 317–325.

Peterson, L., Farmer, J. & Kashani, J. H. (1990). Parental injury prevention endeavors: A function of health beliefs? *Health Psychology*, **9**, 177–191.

Rodin, J. & Salovey, P. (1989). Health psychology. *Annual Review of Psychology*, **40**, 533–579.

Rogers, R. W. (1983). Cognitive and physiological processes in fear appeals and attitude change: a revised theory of protection motivation. In J. T. Cacioppo & R. E. Petty (Eds), *Social Psychophysiology: A Source Book*. New York: Guilford.

Sejwacz, D., Ajzen, I. & Fishbein, M. (1980). Predicting and understanding weight loss: Intentions, behavior and outcomes. In I. Ajzen & Fishbein (Eds), *Understanding Attitudes and Predicting Social Behavior*. Englewood Cliffs, NJ: Prentice-Hall.

Shewry, M. C., Smith, W. C. S. & Tunstall-Pedoe, H. (1990). Health knowledge and behaviour change: A comparison of Edinburgh and north Glasgow. *Health Education Journal*, **49**, 185–190.

Sutton, S. R. & Eiser, J. R. (1990). The decision to wear a seat belt: The role of cognitive factors, fear and prior behaviour. *Psychology and Health*, **4**, 111–123.

Taylor, S. E. (1991). *Health Psychology*, 2nd ed. New York: McGraw-Hill.

Terry, R. D., Oakland, M. J. & Ankeny, K. (1991). Factors associated with adoption of dietary behaviour to reduce heart disease risk among males. *Journal of Nutritional Education*, **23**, 154–160.

The Health of the Nation (1991). London: HMSO.

Townsend, J. (1990). *Price and Income Elasticity of Demand, Taxation and the Smoking Epidemic (1990)*. Harlow, UK: Medical Research Council.

Trichopoulou, A. D. & Efstathiadis, P. P. (1989). Changes of nutrition patterns and health indicators at the population level in Greece. *American Journal of Clinical Nutrition*, **49**, 1042–1047.

Wardle, J. & Steptoe, A. (1991). The European Health and Behaviour Survey: Rationale, methods and initial results from the United Kingdom. *Social Science and Medicine*, **33**, 925–936.

Weinstein, N. D. (1988). The precaution adoption process. *Health Psychology*, **7**, 355–386.

WHO MONICA (1988). Geographical variation in the major risk factors of coronary heart disease in men and women aged 35–64 years. *World Health Statistics Quarterly*, **41**, 115–140.

WHO MONICA (1989). The WHO MONICA Project: A worldwide monitoring system for cardiovascular diseases. *World Health Statistics Annual*, 27–149.

WHO (1989). Causes of death. In *World Health Statistics Annual*. Geneva: WHO.

Index*

---

* Page numbers all refer to the numbering in square brackets at the head of each page.